CYPRUS
THE PRICE OF FREEDOM:

CYPRUS
THE PRICE OF FREEDOM:
An Individual Encircled by Violence Becomes a
Voice for Reconciliation and Peace

STAHIS S. PANAGIDES, PH.D

CITIOFBOOKS, INC.
3736 Eubank NE Suite A1
Albuquerque, NM 87111-3579
www. citiofbooks. com

Hotline: 1 (877) 389-2759
Fax: 1 (505) 930-7244

Ordering Information:
Quantity sales. Special discounts are available on quantity purchases by corporations, associations, and others. For details, contact the publisher at the address above.

Printed in the United States of America.

ISBN-13:   Paperback   978-1-962366-79-3
            eBook   978-1-962366-80-9

Library of Congress Control Number: 2023921098

Contents

NOTE: The reader unfamiliar with the Cyprus problem will benefit in understanding and appreciating this remarkable book by referring to:

• Cyprus History: *https://en.wikipedia.org/wiki/History_of_Cyprus*

• EOKA: *https://www.nam.ac.uk/explore/cyprus-1954-2017*

• EOKA: *https://en.wikipedia.org/wiki/EOKA*

• *https://www.youtube.com/watch?v=bAwto68jEuI&ab_channel=TheUrbanGuide*

INTRODUCTION

I am pleased to have made possible the publication of this book in English based on my late brother's book "ΠΙΚΡΟΔΑΦΝΕΣ" [Bitter Leaves of Laurel]: *Encounters and experiences from the Struggle to free Cyprus from British Colonial Rule and experiences during the first Cyprus House of Representatives 1954-74.*

It is a book set in Cyprus that left many scars and a bitter legacy to Cypriots. It is a book full of anecdotes, memories, and events, and, most importantly, reflections on those events. In his life journey, Dafnis evolved from patriot/terrorist to internationalist/humanist. His religiousness developed from the confines of orthodox Cyprus to the all-embracing positive values of Christianity. His patriotism shifted from a narrow, fanatic Greekness to an appreciation of Hellenic culture's universality.

Dafnis vividly describes his role in The National Organization of Cypriot Fighters (EOKA) and the armed campaign to free Cyprus from British colonial rule, including the hiding in his home of EOKA's leader, George Grivas.

As a pacifist-Christian in a microcosm of religious warriors, Dafnis stood out as a brilliant exception. His personal renunciation of violence was sealed by a question which a shepherd once asked him: "If Jesus was our Archbishop, would he spill blood for the freedom of Cyprus?"

In the years that followed Independence, Dafnis became a reluctant Member of Parliament, disillusioned by Makarios' duplicity and former EOKA combatant's corruption, the poisoned relations between GreekCypriots and Turkish-Cypriots, and among Greek-Cypriots themselves. He comments on many peace plans for Cyprus's political future before and after Independence and laments Cypriots' rejection. Resigning from Parliament for the U.S. to pursue his studies, he writes "In 1966, I decided to resign from the Cyprus House of Representatives to travel to the United States for the opportunity to attend University since, when at an earlier time I could have attended, I was the 'guest' of Queen Elizabeth in Omorphita and Kokkinotrimithia Detention Camps!"

The important message from the book is Dafnis' life and experience "Between Violence and Peace." Revealing how, from the violence and distrust between the two Cyprus communities, it is possible to reach peaceful coexistence and cooperation as Cypriots while maintaining their distinct identities, with lessons for Greece – Turkey relations and beyond.

A film production is underway based on the book and Dafnis' incredible life.

Renowned Greek cinematographer Costas Ferris agreed to be the production director, with the film release expected in 2022.

This book would not have been possible without my wife Joy's improvement of my Google-assisted translation of the Greek original. Special thanks also for their editing loving assistance for Richard and Mary Grace White, Marianne and Stanley Miles, Miguel Villela, Lela Panagides, and

Dimis Michaelides. A special thanks to Cyprus-based Thales Panagides for his prompt response to my frequent requests for information.

Stahis Panagides, PhD Dafnis' brother

Bethesda, Maryland, USA

July 2021

"ΠΙΚΡΟΔΑΦΝΕΣ"
[Bitter Leaves of Laurel]

SUBTITLE: «ΤΙ, ΑΠΟ ΔΙΚΗ ΤΟΥΣ ΧΑΘΗΚΑΝ ΟΙ
ΚΟΥΦΙΟΙ ΑΜΥΑΛΟΣΥΝΗ…»
ΌΜΗΡΟΣ, « ΟΔΎΣΣΕΙΑ»

"Because of their own imprudence, they perished."
Homer, Odyssey. (Rhapsody A, 7)

Encounters and experiences from the Struggle to free Cyprus from British Colonial Rule and experiences during the first Cyprus House of Representatives 1954-74.

In memory of my beloved wife, Maroulla, for her significant contribution to Cyprus's liberation struggle. Without her love and support, it would have been impossible for me to author this book.

The cover picture is inspired by my release from prison: My father, among his many interests, maintained a large birdcage with many songbirds. After my 33 months of detention, when he welcomed me home, he opened the cage and released them all to fly to freedom. Since then, when I hear birds chirping in cages, I wonder if they cry for their fate or simply cry to forget their imprisonment.

Foreword

What is true? the question that cannot be definitively answered. Each of us, by defining the term "truth," expresses subjective terms and interpretations. Historical truths and the presentation of historical facts are also subject to personal view.

The historical truth can be acquired from the experiences of historical events and presented without ulterior motives, personal aspirations, or party colors. Share the facts as they were lived, as they were felt, and record them accurately. Every historian of the future will have to depend on these primary historical sources.

My dear Mr. Dafnis S. Panagides, in the example of General

Makrigianni[1],

---

1   Yiannis Makriyannis (1797–1864), was a Greek merchant, military officer, politician and author, best known today for his Memoirs. Starting from humble origins, he joined the Greek struggle for independence, achieving the rank of general and leading his men to notable victories. Despite his important contributions to the political life of the early Greek state, General Makriyannis is mostly remembered for his Memoirs. Aside from being a source of historical and cultural information about the period, this work has also been called a "monument of Modern Greek Literature", as it is written in pure Demotic Greek. Its literary quality led Nobel laureate Giorgos Seferis to call Makriyannis one of the greatest masters of Modern Greek prose.

gives us his personal firsthand experience in the difficult years of the historical journey of this afflicted and blessed Island, years that have defined and continue to define and shape the future and the course of our homeland; years of hard times, years of struggle, mistakes, and omissions. The lessons learned during this period must allow us to plot a survival course and preserve our people. From the author's experiences, the reader can discern the right and true struggle, the selflessness of the people struggling for their homeland's freedom, and their mistakes and weaknesses. Some of them were deliberately made through human frailties and shortcomings. What matters is that with this book, we have real historical events in our hands because the author shares with honesty what he observed and lived through.

The author, Mr. Panagides, presents things that will bring him no gain in reputation. On the contrary, some of what he writes may disturb a few. A genuine and real person will say things by name, and Dafnis does just that.

The past mistakes must be eliminated and corrected through the "we" and not the "I," which was how our Nation advanced in its glorious history. When the "I" prevailed, it brought about havoc and suffering to our people.

May the Lord, who is the Truth, give this martyred land redemption and enlightenment to properly and wisely manage this redemption. To that end, this book is a significant contribution.

Archimandrite Gennadios

Abbot of the Holy Monastery of Archangel Michael,

Monagri, Cyprus

WHY THIS BOOK WAS WRITTEN

Thanks to my late father, Solomon Panagides, My relationship with books began in my early childhood. I grew up among books, and reading books was a mandatory supplement to my siblings' education and upbringing.

Soon after I graduated from high school, I applied for a loan from the National Bank of Greece, which, at the time, was located at the Central Post Office Square in Limassol. I was asking for a twenty-pound loan to build beehives. I had taken a beekeeping course at the Morphou Agricultural School and a correspondence course in beekeeping from an American University. I saw beekeeping as a professional opportunity. The Director of the Bank was Nikos Mandrid, an uncle of my friend, Eugene Kotsapas, who, to help me, had put in a good word to his uncle about me. "But how did you think this up, Daphne, this unusual job?", the Bank Director asked me with a slightly peculiar look and continued, "After so many years at the bank, I've never had a case like this before."

I answered: "In what other business do you have 250,000 recruits working for free, gathering up and making honey?" He seemed impressed by my reply and listened with interest to my answers to his many questions about bees. He gave me a form and said, "Then let us proceed to the Declaration of Assets." I filled it out and listed: A "Ranch" brand bicycle of post-war construction worth 25 shillings and 1200 volumes of books that I estimated was worth about 350 pounds. The bike, a gift from my father, was very dear to me. I had just learned to ride it, and I was looking for a reason to venture out beyond the remote orchard farm where we lived. I had permission from my father to ride east to the Germasogeia River and west to the "Bathkeia" stream, where the Hotel Crown Plaza is now located.

"Do you have any real estate?" Mr. Mandritis continued, speaking in a language incomprehensible to me. Reading my embarrassment, he asked me to bring a qualified guarantor for the loan.

"I accept the bike," he had said, "but the books, for the bank, have zero value. If they were newspapers, I could accept them because Herodotus, the grocer, uses the paper to wrap olives, cheese, and halva, and that would have some value. But, my dear Daphne, who cares about books?" To my horror, Mr. Mandrid took his red pen and, with a stroke, deleted the books as an asset.

Herodotus Ellinas had a grocery store on Saripolou Street and had gained the trust of the middle-class ladies of Limassol with his smile and pleasant personality. He was also the godfather of my brother, Stahis, and we maintained close family ties.

With the 22-pound salary he was making from his position as Secretary of the Metropolis, my father was always in debt to Herodotus. He often requested Herodotus to give his needy students some food and put it on his account. On one occasion, Herodotus took him aside, saying to him:

"Compadre, you spend too much on children who are not your own. Have you thought about what you're going to leave your children?" His answer: "My Name," 'Solomon Panagides!'. A substantial heritage![2]

I returned to my home, disappointed. It was from that disappointment that was born my strong desire to leave a written record. This wish became more pronounced when I learned that in Talmudic philosophy, for a mortal to be considered a happy man, he must leave behind three things: children, planted trees, and to have written a book.

This book covers a period of 20 years, from 1954 to 1974, a period that marks the modern history of our country, full of dramatic events, events that shaped the present and conditioned the future of our homeland, and during which, circumstances brought me to be an active participant and a firsthand witness.

It was a period that saw the Liberation Struggle of The National Organisation of Cypriot Fighters (EOKA) in 1955-1959[3], the Independence of Cyprus, the first Cypriot House of Representatives, the collapse of the ZurichLondon Agreements, divisions, political assassinations, the Greek junta, the family while an uncle paid for his schooling at a renowned church school in Larnaca. He earned a scholarship at this school from the Bishop of Kition, Meletios Metaxakis. He graduated with honors. Metaxakis, later Patriarch of Constantinople, hired him as his secretary. He was ordained a priest by Bishop Nikodemos Mylonas, whom he also served as a personal secretary. He was one of the two Cypriot teachers who responded to the call of Eleftherios Venizelos to serve

---

[2] Solomon Panagides (1892–1964). He was born in Varosha / Famagusta. His father abandoned the family. His mother worked as a house cleaner to support
[3] https://en.wikipedia.org/wiki/Cyprus_Emergency

[1921–23] in the recently liberated frontier town of Griva, in Macedonia. It is at this time that the Thessaloniki Police Archives described him as "Solomon Panagides, teacher from Cyprus, a dangerous Venizelian [at the time the progressive Prime Minister of Greece] and fervent democrat". During the first Cyprus uprising, in October 1931, seeking the Union of Cyprus with Greece, the British Colonial Government placed him under house arrest at Kalo Chorio, as punishment for his patriotic speech in the funeral of a 15-year-old protester killed by the government forces. Solomon Panagides, while a teacher at Kalo Chorio, founded the first Cyprus Wine Producers Cooperative in 1923.

He was also the founder of the first Sunday Schools and the Orthodox Christian Youth Union (OXEN), as well as the first to organize the institution of summer camps for youth in Cyprus. He also served as a teacher at the Lanition Gymnasium of Limassol.

EOKA B, a coup d'état, and the Turkish invasion the summer of 1974. During this same period, intense diplomatic activities for a solution to the Cyprus problem and much more constitute these years' historical and political context. On all these events, much has been written. In this book, I avoid, where I can, repeating things that have been written by others. For my part, I focus on events for which I have personal experience and describe them exactly as I saw them and as I understood them. Where I consider it appropriate, I borrow from relevant writers and from the testimonies of reliable sources, some of which are coming to light for the first time in this writing.

Readers will notice that there are differences in the description of the same events by the various writers. Some will also point out omissions and imperfections in my book, but I assure them that they are not intentional. Naturally, the passage of time has left its mark. Even the Holy Scriptures, referring to the same facts, present differences in their descriptions. What matters is that the essence of the historical event remains intact.

The book can be viewed as a personal confession. For sure, in many cases, I will be accused of being unduly judgmental because of the disappointment and bitterness which pervades me because of where we have now arrived. And, yes, paraphrasing Kazantzakis, I assume my share of responsibility. But I do not endorse the prevailing view that others are the cause of our problems, whether they are called Anglo-Americans, Communists, Makarios, or Grivas, and more. The responsibility for our predicament is collective. Everyone has their share: some with their actions, others with indifference or inaction, and others with the conscious undermining of the struggles of the Cypriot people. That is why I set the subtitle of my book in the Homeric:

"Because of their imprudence, they have perished."

We experienced an epic struggle for freedom; blood was shed, children were orphaned, mothers lost their children, wives lost husbands, and 200,000 plus our compatriots became refugees. In his book, The Image of the Future, Dutch sociologist Fred Polak argues that the way citizens perceive their country's past determines their country's future. What they expect from their country becomes a self-fulfilling prophecy. In our case, the initial optimism was the promise Makarios made in a speech he delivered from the Archdiocese balcony on March 1, 1959, when he returned from exile to make Cyprus the "State of God."

Themistocles Dervis, then mayor of Nicosia, added his own characterization. We are not "to be the 'State of God' but rather a state of 'the wrath of God'," his answer to Makarios.

Even though there were many accomplishments, such as membership in the European Union, the mismanagement of the state leading to the collapse of banks, such as the Laiki, and the demise of the socially important Cooperative Movement, cronyism, nepotism, and political privileges and favors brought public companies such as Cyprus Airways to ruin. Public works, especially at the local municipal levels, were stained by corruption and much more.

The truth is not always pleasant. Inevitably some will not be pleased by my dismal assessment of our situation. But I do not write to win or lose friends, nor to be liked. Nor is it my intent to tear down or praise idols and events that left deep wounds on our land. I relate events as I lived them. I may sometimes seem severe in my judgment of people that I have loved and with whom I have cooperated, endangering my very life and that of my family. But I follow Aristotle:

"Plato is my friend, but the truth is a better friend."

Because I refer to persons who are no longer alive, I may be accused of judging persons who cannot defend themselves. But we are judged by what we have said, what we have written, and how we have acted. I will leave the conclusion to the reader.

The first three chapters of the book are narratives of what took place. I relate the historical-political events as I have experienced them to help the reader or the historian with my firsthand knowledge of what I saw and lived through.

The last chapter is an analysis of the facts, presenting suggestions regarding the future. My insights and conclusions are undoubtedly influenced by my own values and beliefs, where subjective judgments are inevitable. My aim remains to share the historical truth, not personal gains. Individuals record historical events, analyze them, and present them according to the narrator's personal, ideological, or other sensitivities.

Narrative is, therefore, subjective. Six decades after the Republic of Cyprus's foundation, the Cypriot people are divided when assessing their recent history: Was EOKA a genuine liberation struggle fighting Colonialism, or was it just a rigged imperialist initiative? Some have claimed that the liberation struggle was orchestrated by the CIA and the British secret services! In my opinion, this phenomenon is the symptom of a deep crisis that has eroded our social fabric and divided Cypriot Hellenism, thus leading our Island to the sad state in which we find ourselves.

The crisis's symptoms are not difficult to identify in the whole spectrum of Cypriot life. As citizens, we question our national identity, a people without identity who seek redemption in political party slogans, money, and other ephemeral constructs.

We declare that we are Orthodox Christians, but besides appreciating some frescoed Byzantine churches, in our behavior as individuals, as a society, and as a Church, we are distant from the Orthodox spiritual heritage. Collectively, it is not difficult to see that we suffer from what psychologists call "cognitive dissonance," a serious disease that characterizes people – and I will add, societies with a split personality.

Our conduct and behavior are not consistent with what we say that we are and what we believe. We seek dignity and humanity from our material acquisitions, the stock market, and easy enrichment. Our situation recalls the Jewish people's lament during their Babylonian Exile "By the rivers of Babylon, there we sat, yea, we wept when we remembered Zion."

In today's Cyprus, we are weeping for our occupied land

and lost homes. We look like the cub of the Indian myth. His mother attacked a herd one day. The shepherd killed her, grabbed her little cub, and put it in his flock. The cub grew among the sheep. The more he grew, the more he acted like the other sheep. He lost his identity. While his origins were those of the lion, he worked like a lamb. Growing up, one day, he went to quench his thirst in the water of a lake. That is when he saw himself reflected in the water and wondered:

"But I'm not a sheep. I do not look like the animals in the herd. I'm a lion!"

In the clear water of the lake, the lion discovered his identity. He immediately ran into the forest and joined the other lions.

We, too, need a mirror to rediscover our lost identity.

Looking in our mirror, we stand in admiration for the heroism and self-sacrifice of those who, with their blood, freed us from British subjugation and made us citizens of the European family and a member of the United Nations. But we also lament with the sad song of Marios Tokas, "My homeland has been divided into two, which of the two halves do I love?".

ACKNOWLEDGMENTS

I thank my highly revered and dear friend gennadius, The abbot of the Holy Monastery of Archangel Michael in Monagri in Cyprus, for his hospitality and wise guidance during the book's writing.

Heartfelt thanks also to my friend and fellow EOKA fighter, Pavlos Pavlakis, who has hosted me for many months in his Nissi Beach Hotel and offered me invaluable facilities to focus on the demanding work of writing the book.

The reference to personal experiences of the past inevitably awakens memories. These memories have often created emotional wounds, and they needed to experience professional management, for which I express to Maria Andronicou my great gratitude for her understanding, friendship, and support. Her knowledge and long experience in psychosomatic upkeep have been of crucial importance to me.

It is not possible to separately thank all who helped me in this work. I express my love and gratitude to my children, Lydia, Louisa, Dora, and Thales and their families, my brother Stahis, my friends, and many colleagues. Many are no longer in this life, like my departed dear sister, Chloe. Let their memory be eternal.

I thank God for allowing me at this advanced age of 90 years old to write this book. My ambition is for the book to make a modest contribution to understanding the historical events described.

Dafnis S. Panagides, Limassol, Cyprus, January 2019

CHAPTER ONE

A SUMMARY OF HISTORICAL BACKGROUND:
FROM THE "DESIRABLE" UNION WITH GREECE TO THE
"FEASIBLE" INDEPENDENCE

In this "Politics," Aristotle writes that we must study and understand the past and what brought it about to understand the present. History is an unstoppable flow of events through time. To focus and isolate a historical event, the researcher, without going back and seeing how and why we are here, is, in my opinion, undertaking a frivolous, anti-scientific superficial approach that does not contribute to the objective analysis and understanding of the historical landscape. Examples of such approaches are many in Cyprus. Events with heavy impacts, such as the EOKA struggle for Union with Greece, the coming of Independence, the coup d'état, the Turkish invasion, are such much-discussed historical events, discussed in isolation, often to serve partisan ideological and other interests without examining the events that preceded shaping our present. The period covered by this book will help us understand why we got to where we are. I will refer in some detail to pivotal events that have been central to the course of the Cyprus question[4]

---

[4]https://en.wikipedia.org/wiki/Cyprus_dispute

Hundreds of books have been published on what is referred to as the "Cyprus Problem." The recent history of Cyprus has been described as a "History of Lost Opportunities" (Evangelos Averof), "Course of Doom" (Man. Athanasiou), "Bitter Truths" (Pavlos Diglis), "How We Managed to Come to Zero" (Ploutis Servas), "Cyprus in the Crosshairs" (Dim. Konstantopoulos), "Unfortunate Cyprus" (Savvas Loizides), and others.

The Cyprus struggle for Union with Greece was an expression of the Greek Nation's aspirations formed after the Greek Revolution of 1821, known as the "Great Idea." The Great Idea envisioned the liberation and reintegration of all occupied Hellenic lands in the Ottoman Empire, among which was Cyprus.

Toward this aim, the Church played a decisive role with the archbishop as the "Ethnarch" (Leader and Spokesman of the Ottoman Empire's subject people).

The Struggle for Union with Greece began when Cyprus was still part of the Ottoman Empire, with mostly peaceful demonstrations. It intensified when Cyprus became a colony of the British Crown (1925), culminating in the bloody events of a popular uprising in October 1931.[5]

The demand for Union intensified following the Second World War with the slogan "Union and only Union." The goal had to be achieved "now or never," and it had to be "all or nothing."

The victory of democracies and explicit promises to Greece by its allies and the Cypriots during the Second World War gave new impetus to the Union's prospect. The restoration of the Holy Synod of the Church of Cyprus contributed significantly to the movement with its young,

[5]https://en.wikipedia.org/wiki/1931_Cyprus_revolt

enthusiastic, and newly elected Archbishop, Makarios III, an excellent orator, who followed the uncompromising policy Union of his predecessor Makarios II.

THE GEOPOLITICAL CONDITIONS
WHICH INFLUENCED THE CYPRUS PROBLEM

However, after the end of the Second World War, geopolitical circumstances created new requirements for which Cyprus, due to its geographical position, gained immense importance for the colonial Government and the entire Western world. (See map of Cyprus on page 157)

This critical parameter was not appreciated or evaluated by the political leadership of Greece and Cyprus. Even worse, while the Island's location is its more vital geopolitical negotiating card, its leaders did not take advantage of it at all. It takes no special insight to recognize that Cyprus's geostrategic location has been the decisive factor in its destiny through the ages.

It is worth noting the main prevailing geopolitical conditions of the time:

- The emergence of the desire for freedom and self-determination and the collapse of colonization.

- The Cold War between the countries of Europe and America, on the one hand, and the Soviet Union and the Iron Curtain countries on the other. Simultaneously, one saw the creation of military, political and economic pacts and coalitions, such as NATO, the EEC (later the European Union), the SEATO, the Warsaw Pact, the Non-Aligned Movement, and the United Nations.

- The creation in the heart of the Middle East of the

State of Israel in 1947 was followed by the severe rifts between Arabs and Jews, a severe destabilizing factor in the region whose consequences we are still experiencing today.

- The Middle East is of paramount importance for the interests and survival of Europe and America's industrialized countries because of its energy reserves.

- The expulsion of the British from Egypt and the control of the vital Suez Canal by Nasser.

- Britain was harboring and encouraging Turkish chauvinism in a policy of divide and rule.

- After Nazi occupation, a devastating civil war ensued, and Greece was in no position to clash with its Western allies for Cyprus's sake.

In his "Memoirs," General Grivas does not ignore these critical developments. He writes: "…the Middle East developments brought conditions extremely unfavorable for our cause."

But neither he nor Makarios had given importance to these conditions.

Cyprus's Struggle was conducted with nationalistic and religious sentiments as if Cyprus were something unrelated to these developments. And not only that! Cypriots had come to believe that they could, as Cyprus, play a decisive role in shaping the politics of the great powers: the "Bridge between the East and West," as Makarios declared in his speech from the balcony of the Archdiocese on March 1, 1959, when he returned from exile.

THE TURKISH FACTOR

One of the most serious omissions in shaping our national policy was ignoring the fact that Cyprus was ethnically a heterogeneous society, with Turkish-Muslims accounting for 18% of the population. Presenting the EOKA struggle as a national liberation movement, one must bear in mind that this included only the Greek Cypriot majority. The Turkish minority's reactions, plus how the colonial Government used it for its benefit, were key determinants in the chosen strategy's failure.

The distinguished educator, writer, diplomat, and intellectual Dr. Kyriakos Hatziioannou, in his book "The Origin of the Turkish Cypriots and the Cyprus Issue", published in 1976, cites the results of "demographic research that revealed that the majority of today's Turkish Cypriots were Greek Cypriots who had become Muslims." He writes:

> *"The Turkish Cypriots in the large majority are Greek Cypriots who 'stated' that they were Ottomans to avoid the heavy taxes paid by Christians during the Ottoman domination. Others ended up accepting Turkish ethnicity, while some others remained 'crypto-Christians'."*

Hatziioannou supports this position a) in historical writings and statistics, b) in the Christian manners and customs of many Turkish Cypriots, such as participation in Christian ceremonies, pilgrimages, etc., and c) in the fact that many Turkish Cypriots only spoke Greek. For these reasons, according to Hatziioannou, Greeks, and Turks, conscious of their common origins, lived harmoniously.

Fifty years after Hatziioannou's findings, science confirms that mainland Turks have little in common with the Turkish Cypriots. Recent research of the genetic code reveals that Greek and Turkish Cypriots' DNA comes from a common root, and their DNA has little in common with that of mainland Turks who are of Mongolian origin.

We did just the opposite with our intolerance and bigotry, rather than adopting a rapprochement policy and integrating the two communities. We pushed the Turkish Cypriots "brothers and sisters," as they are characterized by the late Hatziioannou, into Turkey's arms. The worrying thing is that we still have the same mistaken view of identifying our native Turkish Cypriots with the newly arrived Turkish settlers.

BRITISH PROPOSALS

The Church intensified the fight for Union with Greece following the end of the civil war in Greece, with a referendum in 1950 confirming the overwhelming desire of Greek Cypriots for Union with "Mother Greece." The British Government tried to undermine the Union movement with the promise of relaxation of Colonialism's autocratic and anti-democratic laws, introducing some freedoms in internal governance in Cyprus. These proposals were presented in 1947 when the Labor Party in Britain came to power.

The new governor of Cyprus, Lord Winster, convened a conference in November 1947, with the promise of a more liberal and progressive regime. The Church rejected the invitation because the proposal explicitly and categorically excluded the Union of Cyprus with Greece. Only eight Greek Cypriots from the left and all Turkish Cypriot leaders accepted the invitation and participated in the conference.

In May 1948, Britain came back with new proposals, which again precluded the Union with Greece. These proposals stated that: "Cyprus belongs to Britain as part of the Commonwealth, and there cannot be any question about this."

Again, the proposals were rejected; only the Turkish Cypriots kept a positive stance. With the support of the conservative right, the Church replied that they were only willing to discuss the option of Union with Greece.

THE CYPRIOT LEFT JOINS WITH THE CHURCH (ETHNARCHY)

An especially important development with significant consequences was the abandonment by the Communist Party of Cyprus (AKEL) of its aim for Self-determination, in order to join the Church in the quest for Union with Greece. Self-determination was recognized as a universal right, and it was time for it to be recognized for the Cypriots. In a referendum organized by the Church in January of 1950 for Self-determination, with the final aim of Union with Greece, 95% of the Greek Cypriots voted for Union. With an 82% Greek majority being the dominant ethnicity, it was assumed such a dominant majority was to govern while respecting the 18% minority Turkish Cypriots' rights, as happens in democratic regimes. Unfortunately, we have ignored that today. The terms are reversed and we are a minority when we include the 80 million mainland Turks in the population equation!

A secret meeting preceded the AKEL change of strategy from Selfdetermination to Union with Greece at the Bulgarian border in October 1948. Fifi Ioannou and Andreas Ziartidis, executives of AKEL, met with Nikos Zachariades, Secretary of the Communist Party of Greece (KKE).

Andreas Ziartidis was Secretary of the Pancyprian Labour Federation (PEO) and was considered the second in command of Cyprus's communist movement.

In an interview with Panikos Paionides, Andreas Ziartides described their meeting with Nikos Zachariades as follows:

> "...Fifis gave Zachariades a brief manuscript explaining our position. He spoke for about fifteen minutes, explaining our problem. After Nikos Zachariades spoke no more than seven minutes, I think it would be too much if I say ten minutes. He told us that we had committed a mistake cooperating with the British. 'It is wrong,' he said, 'for the Greek people to be fighting, with weapons in hand, against the reactionaries of Greece and their British imperialist allies, and for you in Cyprus to cooperate with the British; your policy must be changed. You must fight for the Union of Cyprus with Greece. We are confident of our victory, and when we win, it will be the solution to your problem'."

After they met with Zachariades, Fifis went to Bucharest to get the opinion of Cominform, which was then the Coordinating Information Office of all the Communist Parties. While waiting for several days for Cominform's views without success, he returned to Cyprus, informing the AKEL leadership of their meeting with Nikos Zachariades. In the meantime, Andreas Ziartidis went to London to get the opinion of the Communist Party of Great Britain. As he said in the same interview mentioned above when he informed the

Secretary-General of the U.K. Communist Party, Harry Pollitt (1890-1960), about their meeting with Nikos Zachariades, he replied: "These views are nonsense. You must work with the English to gradually achieve Union".

While waiting for the return of Ziartidis to Cyprus, the Central Committee of AKEL abandoned the British supported policy of self-government and identified completely with the policy of the Church and the motto "Union= Ένωση."

I refer in detail to this historic decision by the AKEL to fully join with Ethnarchy because I consider it paramount for the subsequent course and the result of the Cyprus struggle for freedom.

In Cyprus, we see a strange coalition of the conservative right represented by Ethnarchy, with the supposed "progressive" left. This symbiosis lasted for almost half a century. In the cooperation of these two extreme ideologies, I attribute the tragic predicament we find ourselves in today. This sad situation has a political and social dimension, as AKEL is equally responsible for the course of our national problem. This strange "marriage" helped absolve the Church from being solely responsible for our impasses not having been solved after fifty years of negotiations. The support of the Church policy from the right and the left gives a unique dimension of universal collective responsibility by society. The argument that is often asserted that others are to be blamed for our situation does not stand because the enemy was and is, ultimately, ourselves.

The culmination of this strange alliance is AKEL's position to go so far as to support Makarios in the "Olive Branch" policy to those responsible for the 1974 EOKA B coup d'état.[6]

---

[6]https://en.wikipedia.org/wiki/EOKA_B

The assertion that AKEL bears responsibility for our dire present predicament and national disaster is not mine. I borrowed it from Ploutis Servas, a man of admirable political acumen and insight.[7]

MY VISIT WITH PLOUTIS SERVAS

I visited Ploutis in March of 1997. He lived near the Cyprus Radio Building.

After many years of my absence abroad, I went to thank him for the touching condolence letter he had sent me when my father died in 1964. Ploutis was expelled from AKEL and worked as an employee of Pavlides & Araouzos Ltd to survive, an ironic twist of history. Pavlides represented General Motors in Cyprus, a colossus of American capitalism. As a founding member of the Communist Party of Cyprus and mayor of Limassol, he had an intense ideological

[7]Ploutis Servas (Πλουτής Σέρβας in Greek; 22 May 1907 – 14 February 2001), was a Cypriot former politician, reporter, and author. Servas was born Ploutarhos Loizou Savvidis (Πλούταρχος Λοΐζου Σαββίδης) and changed his surname to Servas while still a student in secondary education.

Servas was born in Limassol, Cyprus in 1907. He studied social sciences in Moscow and returned to Cyprus in the 1930s. He became the Founder and First General Secretary of AKEL (1941–1945). He was also elected Mayor of Limassol in 1943–1946 and 1946–1949. As the mayor he participated in the consultative assembly and advocated for accepting the British plan of self-government for Cyprus in 1948. For that opinion he became isolated within his party and was expelled in 1952.

confrontation with my father in the time's charged climate. Feelings were so intense that when my late professor at the Greek High School of Limassol, Nikolas Xioytas, was elected member of the Ploutis' Communist leaning Municipal Council, my father had me transferred to another high school, known as "Lykeio Matsakis." I was a fourth-grade student at the Greek Gymnasium of Limassol, and what brought about this sudden transfer was my mentioning to my father that Professor Nicholas Xioutas spoke to us about "someone named Freud!'" "WHAT did he tell you about Freud in class?" My father asked. "Tomorrow, you'll be enrolled in a different high school." For Solomon Panagides, sexual education was part of the Sunday School curriculum that he first founded in Cyprus. The only sex education books we could read were Anna Katsigras's *Sexual Education for the Boy*, and *Sexual Education for Girls*, and Tihamer Toth's *Pure Youth*.

"What do you think of the political situation, my dear Daphne?" Ploutis asked me by putting his hand on my shoulder. "You're the person responsible for what happened," I replied. My answer surprised him. "But how dare you say that. Didn't you read my books?"

"I say it exactly because I read you, and you bear all the responsibility because you didn't become Archbishop."

I referred to his book "When We Were Children", where he wrote about when his grandmother would give him a dime to bring bread from the neighborhood bakery that was often their only food for the day. When he handed her the bread, she would give him her blessing: "Have my blessing, my son, and I hope one day to see you as the Archbishop."

He was flattered by my comment; he put his arms around me and kissed me.

"But let's talk seriously," he said. "The Gold Medal of the

Destruction of Cyprus, I award to Hezekiah Papaioannou, in other words to AKEL, and to Makarios I give the silver."[8]

"And to the General (Grivas)?" I asked.

"Let us give him the bronze. But the responsibility lies with those who make the political decisions. Not the military who implements them."

I left Ploutis Servas deeply troubled. He was endowed with a great sense of political understanding, and his diagnosis was insightful. AKEL's Stalinist, fiercely anti-Western orientation was one main reason that led to the tragedies that we experienced. Following the Zurich Agreements, AKEL and the Church, the political-religious establishments of Cyprus, remained in close cooperation. They determined Cyprus' foreign policy as well as the contours of internal governance. These policies are the primary reasons for the Turkish occupation and today's economic and social crisis.

The policies that defined the future of Cyprus were, in my view: a) Resort to an armed struggle against the English with clearly ethnocentric criteria without taking into consideration the Turkish Cypriots, and b) the turning our backs on the West, tying Cyprus to the so-called NonAligned Nations camp.

For the espousing ethnocentrism, the Church bears the responsibility, and for the turning of our backs to the West, the Communist AKEL bears the full responsibility.

---

[8] https://en.wikipedia.org/wiki/Ezekias_Papaioannou

INDEPENDENCE WILL NEVER BE GRANTED TO CYPRUS

This statement from the British Deputy Minister of Colonies was decisive in the development of the Cyprus problem. Henry Hopkinson, addressing the British House of Representatives on July 28 1954, stated, "For some colonies, including Cyprus, the right to self-determination will never be granted."

The "Never" of Hopkinson provoked strong protests in Britain, Greece, and Cyprus. In a letter dated October 22 1954 from the Conservative MP and Executive of the Intelligence Service, Dick Bowman, to the Minister of the Colonies, Lennox Boyd, writes warning of denying Cyprus the right to Independence from colonial rule. He wrote: "You have ruled out every peaceful way, and there will be bloodshed. You will mourn your children and us, our brothers" (Robert Holland, *Never Land: British Colonial Policy and the Roots of Violence in Cyprus* 1950-54, page 148).

Meanwhile, appeals to the U.N. from Greece to recognize the principle of self-determination for the Cypriots were voted down in the U.N. General Assembly, under Anglo objections and strong opposition from Turkey.

CYPRUS ENTERS THE ARMED STRUGGLE

Under these circumstances, the initial reservations about the use of armed violence by Makarios and a small group of Government and military agents in Athens were surmounted. Cyprus entered decisively toward an armed liberation struggle.

The original intention was to "create noise" with a few explosions, to let people know that Cyprus exists as General George Grivas – Digenis, who took responsibility for organizing and conducting the armed independence struggle, wrote in his memoirs.

Digenis presented his "Preliminary Plan of Revolutionary Action in Cyprus," which formulated the Struggle's purpose. He wrote:

> *"By acts of heroism and self-sacrifice to bring about the interest of international public opinion and the Allies themselves, to the Cyprus question ... By continuing serious harassment of the British in Cyprus ... we will not forsake sacrifice, but on the contrary, we will proceed until we achieve our goal. The Struggle will continue until International Diplomacy-UN, and the English especially, are forced to examine the Cyprus question and immediately give a solution, following the aspirations of the Cypriot People and the whole of the Greek Nation."*

TURKS AND **AKEL** DENOUNCE THE **EOKA** STRUGGLE

The armed Struggle, which began on April 1 1955 and continued to March 1958, was given much publicity, demonstrating heroic patriotism in Greek history's best valiant examples. The sacrifice and heroic feats of EOKA fighters cultivated national pride in Cyprus and Greece. The people were united behind Archbishop Makarios, their political leader, and George Grivas, the military commander.

However, and although our side did not pay attention, the Turkish Cypriots' reaction immediately after the start of the armed liberation struggle was significant. A Bi-communal polarization emerged, exploited by the U.K. government assuming the role of the intercommunity mediator.

Dr. Fazil Kutchuk, Secretary of the Turkish Cypriot National Party (Vice-President of the Republic of Cyprus after the signing of the ZurichLondon agreements), sent a telegram to the Minister of the Colonies, Lennox Boyd, and to the Governor, Robert Armitage,[9] expressing concern about the April 1st eruptions. The Turkish Cypriots' reaction against EOKA was continuous and in close cooperation with the British occupying forces.

On June 30, 1955, a leaflet in the Turkish language was published in Limassol, inviting the Turkish youth to join the ranks of a secret Turkish Cypriot group to "fight EOKA and abort the Union of Cyprus with Greece."

EOKA replied with a leaflet in the Turkish language, released in Limassol's Turkish sector in July 1955. Among other things, the flyer stated:

"Our intentions towards the Turkish inhabitants of the Island are wholesome and one of friendship. We want to remain genuine friends and allies, and as far as we are concerned, we will not harm in the least your dignity, life, honor, and property."

---

[9]https://en.wikipedia.org/wiki/Robert_Perceval_Armitage

A hostile attitude towards the EOKA struggle was also expressed, at the time, by the leadership of AKEL. The AKEL leadership addressed, in vulgar language, both Digenis and the fighters of EOKA.

Many AKEL members disagreed with the leadership of the party. They founded their own organization called "Organization of Left-Wing Nationalists" with the participation of left-wing organizations such as PEO (Pancyprian Labor Federation) and others.

But in the course of the EOKA struggle, actions that took place either because of an organized challenge by Turkish nationalists or excessive zeal of Greek Cypriots shook the confidence of the Cypriots, contributing to the climate of mistrust and insecurity that characterizes both sides still today.

In his book, "The AKEL Leadership and the Armed Struggle-Marxist Critique", "Democritus" strongly criticized AKEL's leadership for its attitude toward the EOKA liberation struggle. "Democritus" was the nickname of Gogos Cacoyannis, a respected jurist of Limassol and an important member of AKEL, who kept in touch with EOKA and offered important services to the liberation struggle, including the hiding in his home of the EOKA Limassol leader, Demos Hatzimirtis, assuming tremendous personal risk. Under the emergency laws, such cooperation with EOKA was punishable by death.

The "Organization of Left-Wing Nationalists" 'released leaflets critical of AKEL's leadership. A leaflet released on February 18, 1958, said, among other things, that "We have evidence that clearly shows that the order [by the AKEL leadership] not just to harass the masked [EOKA fighters] but to beat them, is cause for the last unfortunate and sad events that cost the lives of some of our children."

In another leaflet released on March 11, 1958, the "Organization of Left-Wing Nationalists" entitled "Them and Us" states:

> *"...It is time to put an end to this anti-ethnic, anti-Marxist action of our [AKEL] leadership. It is time to reveal their appalling behavior, denounce them, and join with the other struggling Cypriot people in a united fighting front [for the liberation of Cyprus]. Even now, at this late hour."*

Under massive popular pressure and internal dissent, the Central Committee of AKEL, in March 1957, revised the party's stance towards the EOKA liberation struggle. That decision stated, among other things:
"...At the same time, the Central Committee underlines that in our attitude towards EOKA, we committed several mistakes, some of which are quite serious."

Self-criticism is admirable, which shows why AKEL overcame serious inter-party crises while other parties from the right were dissolved.

The George Grivas and the Communists' ideological rivalry has been diachronic and the AKEL occasional representatives not missing the opportunity to criticize him as bully in EOKA, plus a murderer, a fascist, and worse.

Here we must note to help better understand AKEL's negative attitude towards General Grivas by recalling his decisive role in the Greek communists' defeat in the Athens Battle of the Thission in 1944 during the Greek Civil War. The defeat of the communists in that battle derailed establishing a government in Greece allied with the Soviet Bloc.

BRITISH INITIATIVES MAKARIOS' MEETING WITH GOVERNOR-GENERAL HARDING

One of the most serious developments in Cyprus's thorny course of recent history, and the most important, was the Makarios-Harding meeting at the Holy Monastery of Kykkos on January 28 1956.

General Grivas was hiding in the forest within walking distance from the monastery with his team of fighters, where Makarios and Harding discussed Cyprus's future.

Grivas was under the impression that the two would end in Agreement. After thanking the rebel group for contributing to the Struggle, he posed for the unique commemorative photo in his military uniform. He told his team that they were to receive a small amount of money to buy a suit and present themselves to their families.

Marshal Harding gave a letter to Makarios, in which Great Britain recognized the right of the people of Cyprus to self-determination.

Makarios Drousiotis, in an article published in the newspaper Politis on February 15, 2009, entitled "50 Years Since the Signing of the Zurich London Agreements: Five Seconds that Judged the Future of Cyprus," says:

> "...After three years of killing and divisions between the Greeks and Turks, left and right, we accepted a far worse solution than the one rejected in 1956. Today, it is widely accepted that the Harding proposal was a missed opportunity, which would lead to single Independence or even to the Union"

and continues in the same article:

"Makarios's talks with Harding resulted in a draft declaration that the Government would make in the House of Commons and describe the general principles of the new status of Cyprus. Makarios was positive. He met in the mountain the military leader of EOKA George Grivas and informed him. Grivas announced to the rebels who were with him that their fight was over. They all took a commemorative picture together. It is the famous photo of Grivas on the mountain, surrounded by his men."

WITH MAKARIOS

British colonial Minister, Lennox-Boyd, arrived in Cyprus on February 29, 1956, to meet with Makarios and secure his final consent. Makarios had no intention of interrupting the talks and rejecting the proposal. But before he said yes, he sought to test his interlocutors, the "Synod," the highest authority of the Church of Cyprus.

Makarios greeted Lennox-Boyd with an unpleasant surprise. Despite the ceasefire held by EOKA because of the talks, Nicosia was shocked by 19 bomb explosions just before the meeting began. Makarios blamed the blasts on Grivas, while Grivas blamed the initiative on Makarios, who wanted, before the final Compromise, to send a "strong message" to Lennox-Boyd, obviously to get more."

In a conversation with the late Tassos Papadopoulos, when he was Minister of Labour and Social Insurance, and I was a member of the House of Representatives, he told me that in his question to Makarios on why he rejected the Harding proposals, he replied: "When I informed my brothers in Christ of the English proposals, they replied: 'Self-determination in 7-10 years; they should have given it to us yesterday. We do not accept anything less, Self-determination now.'"

The 19-bomb explosion in Nicosia on February 29, 1956, marked the final shipwreck of the negotiations. Whoever gave instructions for this provocative activity still divides us. One of the accomplices fled to England.

Many lay the responsibility onto Makarios, claiming that the bombs came out of the Archdiocese. Others attribute this to Grivas and others to the British military, who wanted to continue operations against EOKA to rescue the suffering prestige of Great Britain.

I had not seen convincing evidence about who bears the responsibility for the explosions, disobeying Digenis' order for a Cyprus-wide truce. I am surprised when I read serious analysts who conclude, despite uncertainty, that it was either Makarios or Grivas. I am not superstitious, but history seems to have played a uncanny game — February 29, 1956, was a Leap Year!

Lennox-Boyd, annoyed by Makarios's attitude and outraged by the explosions, interrupted the talks and said goodbye to Makarios with the well-known phrase "God save your people." Makarios took it as a wish, but in his mind, the British Minister knew the draconian measures the British would take to quell EOKA.

As the first such measure, on March 9, 1956, the English exiled Makarios to the Seychelles Islands in the Indian Ocean, along with Metropolitan Kyprianos of Kyrenia, Papa Stavros Papagathagelou, and Polykarpos Ioannides. They remained in exile until March 28, 1957, when they were released. They were not allowed to return to Cyprus and settled in Greece.

In Cyprus, the EOKA struggle was at its peak, while the English had intensified their efforts to crush EOKA, which was internationally damaging to Great Britain's prestige. In addition to the large-scale military operations to locate Digenis, they applied cruel and horrific torture to obtain information from members of the organization, that could have led to the EOKA Leader's arrest. They offered large sums to informants, and it is a fact that the organization did suffer losses from informants. But the oppressive measures hardened the resistance of the Cypriot people even more. In the basement of the Foreign Office in London, there are many boxes with documents relating to the EOKA struggle, which have not yet been opened. The researcher and author, Leonidas Leonidou, found some of the crates, bear the following marking: "List of informants by province, city, and community. To open in the year 2080".

The Ethnarch Makarios was anxious about Cyprus's situation, isolated as he was in distant Seychelles. According to testimonies from his fellow detainees, he became concerned whether the armed Struggle's continuation would be in the Cyprus people's interest. He had previously rejected all the British proposals, which provided some relaxation of the oppressive colonial rule, and promised to apply self-determination principles in the future.

BRITISH PROPOSALS-RADCLIFFE

In December 1956, the chief Prosecutor of Cyprus, Kriton Tornaritis, and a representative of the Foreign Office visited Makarios in the Seychelles. They asked to see him alone and away from the other exiles. They had with them the new proposals of the British Government for Cyprus known as "The Radcliffe Plan" and wanted to personally explain it to him.

Radcliffe had arrived in Cyprus on July 15, 1956, to personally investigate the situation and submit suggestions for compiling a constitution for the Cypriot people's self-government. For the Greeks of Cyprus, the dictum was not to carry any negotiation without Makarios' presence. Turkish Cypriot politicians with Fazil Kutcuk, following a more pragmatic policy, collaborated closely with the English Constitutional specialist stressing that the future Constitution should provide for the two communities' parity. Radcliffe left for London on August 2, 1956.

He returned to Cyprus in September 1956, but no Greek Cypriots spoke with him. Thus, based on what he found and what the Turkish Cypriot politicians told him, he completed his work and submitted it to the British Minister of the Colonies, Lennox Boyd, on November 12, 1956. The Radcliffe proposals were communicated to the Greek Government by Lennox-Boyd himself, who went to Athens specifically for this purpose.

On December 16, 1956, the Greek Government rejected the Radcliffe Constitution because it was neither liberal nor democratic and was not leading to self-determination nor following the fundamental principles of the U.N.

The Constitution provided a system of double commands where the Governor would have responsibilities for foreign policy, defense, and internal security. Simultaneously, the remaining issues were assigned to the Legislative Council, consisting of 24 Greek Cypriots and six Turkish Cypriots, plus six members representing the Governor.

The Constitution was accompanied by four conditions: a) Cyprus would remain under British sovereignty, b) the British military bases would remain in Cyprus, c) the Governor would be responsible for foreign policy and Internal Security, and (d) the system would be liberal in nature, to ensure self-government with clauses for the protection of minorities.

A large part of the Constitution concerned relations between the two communities. Radcliffe had given enough protection to the Turkish Cypriots but not a numerical upgrade to the legislature, as they had requested.

The equal political representation demanded by the Turks was rejected by Lord Radcliffe in its "constitutional proposals" in 1956. He wrote:

> *"I gave my best attention to the claim that was raised by the Turkish Cypriot community, that they should be granted equal political representation with that of the Greek community ... But this is a claim of 18%, and, if this is to be applied, I think it needs to be justified."* ...
> *"The first encompasses the idea of a federation rather than a unified state. It would be quite natural for the members of a federation to be granted equality of representations in the land, irrespective of the populations' numerical proportions of the territories they represent. But can Cyprus be organized as a federation*

in this way? No, I do not think so. There is no sample of territorial separation between the two communities and, apart from other objections, a federation of communities which does not also include Federation of Territories seems to be a very difficult constitutional form."

Lord Radcliffe concludes in the same paragraph:

"My conclusion is that it cannot be in the interest of Cyprus as a whole to divide the Constitution based on equal political representations of Greek with the Turkish Cypriot community."

THE STATEMENT BY LENNOX BOYD

When Lord Radcliffe testified as to his plan, Lennox-Boyd's Foreign Office considered that there should be a reference to a possibility of partition to give hope for Turkish-Cypriots and discourage the Greek Cypriots from continuing the EOKA struggle. On December 19, 1956, Lennox-Boyd, in the discussion of the Radcliffe Constitution in the British House of Representatives, said:

"The purpose of Her Majesty's Government will be to ensure that the exercise of Self-determination is carried out in such a way that in the Turkish Cypriot community, as in the Greek Cypriot community, the opportunity

*is given, due the peculiar situation of Cyprus,
to decide for itself on its future status.*"

Lennox-Boyd's statement was a turning point for the Cyprus issue, as for the first time, it recognized the Turkish Cypriots' right to self-determination, which could lead to partition. This opening was a British maneuver as a warning to the Greek Cypriots that if they insisted on their right to self-determination, this could lead to partition.

The Greek Government of Konstantinou Karamanlis turned down the plan, while Turkey and the Turkish Cypriots welcomed the Radcliffe project since it opened the way to partition.

In the Seychelles, the talks between Makarios and the envoys of the Foreign Office met with a great deal of disagreement among the exiles, and we can say that it was the beginning of the disastrous division of the Cyprus Hellenism, the division into "Makariakous" – pro-Makarios and "Anti-Makariakous"- Against Makarios. From the unity of the people who led to the epic of 1955-59, a division emerged that led us to the precipice of our national doom.

As a result of this meeting with Lennox-Boyd, Makarios was persuaded that while the "Desirable" was the Union, the "Feasible" was Independence. Great psychological pressure on Makarios to compromise Independence was Lennox-Boyd's statement to the British House of Representatives. If Britain finally accepted the Greek Cypriots' request for self-determination, it had to be applied separately for the Greek Cypriots and Turkish Cypriots. This meant the partitioning of Cyprus, a solution unacceptable to the Greek Cypriots.

The British colonial Minister's statement was not a bluff.

In consultation with Turkey, the English had already prepared a draft of a bi-communal, bi-zonal partition.

Among the United Kingdom documents on Cyprus, a file has a handwritten note (Fo 371/123894) dated May 31, 1956, by the Foreign Office Director-General, Sir Ivan Kirkpatrick, the Council of Ministers. In it, he writes, "If we are forced to announce a solution to the Cyprus problem, we must seriously consider partition." Professor Nihat Erim, an adviser to the Turkish Prime Minister Menderes, in a report to the Turkish Government dated November 24, 1956, recommended the territorial partition, with the circumvention of the democratic principle of majority rule, proposing two separate States with equal political rights. The proposals were accompanied by a plan to implement it with population movement.

To be fair to Makarios, those who blame him for violating his "Faneromeni"[10] oath by abandoning the goal of Union with Greece should appreciate his intention to avoid partition. What he can be accused of is that his later policies and actions contributed to the partition.

Makarios's decision to abandon the objective of Union as desirable and move towards a solution of Independence as a feasible goal was crucial in Cyprus's history.

With this historical background, we reached the Zurich-London agreements, where the Union is denied, and Turkey's rights over Cyprus are recognized. At the same time, Britain retains a large territorial part of the Island, with the anachronistic principle of racial discrimination enshrined in the Constitution.

Makarios and his fellow exiles were released from the

[10] On August 22, 1954, at the Faneromeni Church in Nicosia a nationwide rally was held in which over 50,000 Greeks took the "Faneromeni oath" that was proclaimed by Makarios:

Seychelles on March 28, 1957, by the British Government's decision that forbade them to return to Cyprus.

> *"We're doing well. Do not let anyone get in the way. Let no one betray his principles and beliefs. We are Greeks and with the Greeks we want to live. Under these sacred domes, let today us give the sacred oath: We will remain faithful to death in our national request. No retreats. No concessions. No transactions. We will despise violence and tyranny. We would bravely elevate our morale over small and ephemeral obstacles, not merely pursuing, in the only pursuit of an end, the Union and only the Union [with Greece]."*

Makarios settled in the Hotel Grande Bretagne in Athens, returning to Cyprus on March 1, 1959. The agreements with which Cyprus became a republic were already signed in Zurich and London. In Athens, the other exiles' relations with Makarios were strained, and the Cypriot Hellenism division began to deepen and exacerbate.

A group of Cypriot nationalist students devised a plan to assassinate Makarios in his Athens hotel, but it was eventually abandoned. A decisive role in the cancellation of Makarios's assassination plan was played by the psychiatrist, Dr. Takis Evdokas.

The belief was that the only feasible solution for an independent Cyprus State led to the Zurich London agreements. So, when on March 1, 1959, we heard from Makarios from the gallery of the Archbishopric "Brothers we have won," we were ecstatic, with national pride and hope for the future. I was one of the thousands present who applauded Makarios, our Ethnarch.

Diplomat Giannis Kranidiotis who accompanied Makarios, recalls that Makarios asked him to read his "Return to Cyprus" speech. When Giannis suggested deleting the phrase "Brothers, We Have Won," Makarios reacted negatively to this suggestion, and in a strong tone, informed him that the "Brothers, We Have Won" had to stay.

In his book *Strategic Depth,* Davutoglu considers the signing of the Zurich-London agreements as the biggest victory of Turkish diplomacy since the Treaty of Lausanne was signed on July 24, 1923. Those who ignore history claim that Turkey brought the coup d'état to Cyprus, however treacherous and condemnable the coup d'état was.

The Treaty of Guarantee, which is part of the Zurich-London agreements, remains the biggest obstacle to finding a viable and tolerable solution to the Cyprus problem after more than six decades.

It took only three years to prove that what was "feasible" proved to be "unfeasible." For over five decades, we have been looking for a "workable solution." Recent proposals for a possible solution to date, although not presented as a complete solution to the Cyprus problem, appear to be based on the same or worse stipulations than those of the Zurich Agreements on which in vain we have tried to build the Republic of Cyprus.

Digens orders the end of the armed Struggle

On March 9, 1959, Digenis released a pamphlet declaring the end of the armed struggle of EOKA.

I consider this pamphlet's content to be the most important contribution of EOKA during its four-year Struggle for Cyprus's freedom. It reveals Digenis' high moral standards, his quality of character imbued with authentic, selfless patriotism. This document follows as reported in the Grivas "Memoirs" (p. 403).

> *To the Greek people of Cyprus: When on April 1, 1955, I raised the flag of the Revolutionary Movement, I set out as my purpose the liberation of Cyprus and sought the support of the Greek Cypriot people and the support of the whole Greek Nation, and they were given to me fully during our four-year arduous fight.*
>
> *Now, in light of the Zurich agreement between the governments of Greece and Turkey, ratified by The National Leader [Ethnarch] Makarios, I am obliged to order a ceasefire.*
>
> *The ones who would not accept the Agreement and continue the Struggle would not only divide the Cypriot people, but probably the whole of the Greek Nation, and the results of the National Division would be infinitely more destructive than the shortcomings of the Agreement.*
>
> *In my view, the Agreement, even if it is not the one that we desired, is preferred to national division because everything will be lost in such a division.*

Instead of the call to arms, I call for solidarity, unity, and love, so that the glorious Cypriot people will rebuild the young Republic's edifice on the present ashes. It is up to the leaders to guide us on the path of prosperity and progress.

As far as I am concerned, I am determined not to get involved in Cyprus or Greece's politics and public life. From a distance[11], I will observe the footsteps of my much-tortured and bloody Father Land, sharing with you its joys and pains. I have my conscience clear that I did my duty. It is now the political leaders' responsibility to exploit the epic Struggle the Cypriot people have achieved. We must now be disciplined and rally around the Ethnarch, who symbolizes National unity, and assist him in his difficult work.

---

[11]A promise that he did not keep. With the signing of the Zurich-London agreements in early 1959 and Cyprus's declaration as an independent state, Grivas reluctantly ordered a cease-fire since the struggle's main objective of Enosis was not achieved. His views were at odds with those of Makarios, who had accepted the above agreements on behalf of the Greek Cypriot population. In March 1959, Grivas came out of his hideout and departed (in exile, requested by the UK as part of the cease-fire agreement) for Athens, where he received a hero's welcome as the liberator of the Greek Cypriots and was subsequently decorated with the highest honors by the Greek Parliament and the Athens Academy and promoted to the rank of General. Not long after his return, Grivas was persuaded to enter politics as head of a coalition party but soon abandoned this route after the disappointing percentage his party obtained in the general election of 1963.

This is my wish, and I ask you to follow it.

Digenis, Leader

WE SAY GOODBYE TO GRIVAS

A few days before departing from Cyprus, on March 15, 1959, Digenis invited us to Nicosia to say goodbye. At the House of Socrates Iliadis, we had gathered individuals who had worked with him in one way or another. He wanted to thank us and give us his latest advice. In one room were gathered members of the rebel groups. In the other, in which I was with my wife, Maroulla, and the couple, Marios and Ellis Christodoulou, were the people who helped the Organization "in the background."

After thanking us for our cooperation with him, he repeated that we should unconditionally support Makarios and do whatever he wanted us to do.

At one point, I interrupted him by asking: "But Chief, support him in all that he tells us to do?"

The reply: "Yes, whatever he tells you" - and making a characteristic gesture with both hands and in a bold style, he added: "And do somersaults; if he tells you to do them, do them!"

With such moods and feelings, we began our journey toward the building of the Republic of Cyprus. On March 17 1959, the EOKA leader returned to Greece.

CHAPTER TWO

THE **EOKA** STRUGGLED UP TO THE SIGNING OF THE ZURICH-LONDON AGREEMENTS(1954-1960).

"When the bewildering secret winds began to blow, Cyprus, too, harbored its own secret."

—*July 9, 1821, Vasilis Michaelides*

SOMETHING HAS CHANGED!

No other writing has the strength and vibrancy of vasilis michaelides' description of Cyprus's climate in July 1821. But the hidden winds began to blow again in Cyprus from the day George Grivas Digenis arrived secretly on the Island and landed on the deserted shore of "Aliki" near Chloraka, north of Paphos, the night of November 10, 1954.

I was 25 years old. We lived on our small family farm east of Limassol near the chapel of St. George, known as "Agiorkoydi of Frangoudi." In addition to my wife, Maroulla, with us were my parents: Solomon Panagides, and my mother Maria, known as "Konomissa," and my sister, Chloe, and my brother, Stahis. Staying with us were also my grandfather

Socrates, my Grandma Iphigenia, cousins from the village attending high school, and my father's dedicated assistant for many years, Despinou, known as Kareni. Also staying with us was Pollys Ioannou from the village of Apsiou, who took care of the farm. Workers from the village also stayed with us for a few days assisting with our orchard's seasonal farming necessities. Pollys had served in the Cyprus Regiment during the Second World War and was an active PEO member. He knew of my participation in EOKA, and despite his leftist orientation, he worked closely with me with consistency and confidentiality.

Because of my work (I was an importer of agricultural machinery), a German technician, Mr. Hellmut Zaoyer, stayed with us. Turkish Cypriot customers often visited from many distant places like Lefka, who stayed to dine with us in a climate of friendship and cooperation. When leaving, they respectfully kissed the hand of my priest father, receiving his blessing.

Our neighbors were an English group from a religious fraternity whose leader was the English archaeologist, John Sebastian Marlow Ward[12], considered one of the most controversial early 20th century figures. He was a high-ranking official of the Masonic Lodge, and when in his book he revealed important secrets of Freemasonry, the International Masonic Order decided to exterminate him. He traveled to Syria, where he was ordained an Orthodox bishop. He then returned to England and founded the "Christian Brotherhood of the King of Christ" in East Barnet. A member of the Brotherhood was the daughter of the Director of the great British household electrical appliances industry, Electrolux, who wanted to eradicate the Wards and dissolve their Brotherhood. Ward succeeded in escaping secretly to

[12] https://en.wikipedia.org/wiki/John_Sebastian_Marlowe_Ward

Cyprus, accompanied by 13 followers, and settled on the farm next to ours. He claimed that he and his wife, Mother Mariam, had been communicating with angels who guided the Brotherhood course.

In 1954, I traveled to Germany on business. Correspondence could take fifteen days, and the sending of telegrams was not always easy. Once my wife was worried that she had not heard from me for many days.

"Don't worry, Maroulla," Mother Mariam said. "Tonight, you'll hear from Dafnis."

That same night, Mother Mariam informed Maroulla that I was at a café at the Geneva railway station and was in a good mood and health. As she claimed, she had a vision and spotted me in Geneva. The information that she gave my wife was correct.

A few days before my meeting with Andreas Ioannides and Christakis Tryfonides that introduced me to EOKA and the subsequent armed Struggle in the up to then peaceful and idyllic Cyprus, our neighbor Mariam Ward foretold what was to happen. Following her husband's (Father Ward) death a few months earlier, buried in St. Nicholas' cemetery in Limassol, Mother Ward assumed the Order's leadership. She invited me to their home to announce that the previous night she received a message from the Guardian Angel informing her that soon, Cyprus would burst into great turmoil and the lives of members of the Brotherhood would be in great danger. They had to leave Cyprus as quickly as possible. They sold the farm hastily and left for East Africa. Mother Mariam tried to convince me to follow them but did not persuade me.

About that same time, I sensed a strange change in the behavior of Tryfonides, whom I employed as a tractor driver.

"Christakis," I asked him. "Do you have a problem? Lately, you do not seem to be concentrating on your work. You're often absent-minded and seem to show some secrecy in your movements and words."

"Yes," he tells me. "There is something, but we'll talk later." I figured he was having some family problems.

The next day, late in the afternoon, my (wedding) best man and close friend, Ioannidis, came to the orchard. He had just opened his bookstore on Athens Street. Andreas was remarkably active in the Christian movement and was the Secretary of OXEN (Orthodox Christian Youth Association), whose founder was my father.

"We want to talk to you in private," he said, "and away from the house." We sat under a lemon tree, Ioannidis, Tryfonides, and I.

"It's been a while," Ioannidis began to say. "We are concerned if we should reveal what we are about to tell you now. We are afraid of the close cooperation you have with the English since this is about your initiation into EOKA,[13] the organized anti-colonial Struggle that we started a few months ago. We worry that you may unwittingly tell them about the secrets of our organization, which will have tragic consequences for you - and for the outcome of our fight."

Indeed, I worked in close cooperation with the Department of Agriculture, whose Director and many senior executives were English. The English Director of Agriculture, Kenneth Jones, even offered me a scholarship to the Commonwealth Agricultural Bureau, which I had not accepted for family reasons.

---

[13] https://en.wikipedia.org/wiki/EOKA

I Become a Member of **EOKA**

My talk with Ioannides and Tryfonides lasted a long time. My mother repeatedly called to come to eat, but we continued without interruption. Our orchard was a few kilometers outside the city limits of Limassol, where the population at the time did not exceed 25,000. Only three or four families lived in the surrounding orchards. The orchard was well located and had the potential for many uses, i.e., to hide trainers from Greece, wanted fighters, and weapons.

"Weapons and ammunition?" I was startled. "Where do we get them?

How do we use them?"

"Don't ask too many questions and learn to keep your mouth shut,"

Tryfonides said.

"Count me in," I said. From that moment on, I was a member of the organization...EOKA. "But in an auxiliary role as I cannot kill even a sparrow."

"These are matters which the Uncle decides."

"But what Uncle, you guys? You're making me crazy," I said.

"Pray to God that you learn," said Ioannidis...with humor.

The Limassol EOKA unit was small; we were separated into groups of three people each and were assigned to identify sabotage targets. The instructions were, then, to cause material damage. We had to avoid bloodshed at all costs, and that pleased me. The aim was to arouse the interest of international public opinion and press Great Britain to accept the Cypriot people's demands, which was then the union of

Cyprus with Greece.

Apart from Andreas Ioannides and Christakis Tryfonidis, the members I met were Theodoros Sourmelis from St. Theodore of Agros, and Kosmas Souliotis, Fotis Iakovides, and Georgios Koyllapis from Agios Mamas.

As the first target, we chose to torch the poles of the City Electricity Authority, which had just been unloaded on the beach next to the estuary of "Bathkeias" near the chapel of St. George Fragkoudi. It was a flammable target and unguarded, so success was assured.

In 1955, on April Fools' Day, EOKA launched the beginning of the liberation struggle with the proclamation of Digenis.

It should be noted here that the proclamation did not explicitly state that the purpose of the struggle was to be the Union of Cyprus with Greece. Still, it was declaring its objective to be "the shaking of the English yoke," the first step being the recognition of the right of self-determination for the Cypriot people who, when free, could choose Union with Greece, which was later characterized by Makarios as the "desired" or "possible" goal.

Meanwhile, we sold our old orchard and settled closer to town but again in an area with few inhabitants and accessible only from the dirt road that led to Agios Nikolaos' cemetery. It continued as a dirt road, used mainly by few cars going to Germasogeia village.

Our first action was to build a small hideout to conceal weapons and men who were the "Most Wanted" by the authorities. The first fugitives that we hosted came from Larnaca. They were the EOKA fighters, Kikis Filiastidis and Kokos Olympios. They stayed with us a few days until they received instructions from Digenis to join rebel groups. Another guest at our hideout was Lefkios Rodosthenous following his traumatic escape in September 1955 from the Kyrenia fortress.[14] We hid a couple of revolvers in the small crypt, a few sticks of dynamite, detonators, and an automatic rifle. Upon receiving an order, we would supply ammunition to EOKA in other areas, usually delivered in baskets covered with jasmine or in egg boxes covered with straw. These activities were never discovered by the authorities.

A frequent visitor to the crypt was Sophocles Potamitis, who built homemade grenades using pipe fittings, mines, and other explosive devices, and then training members to use such ammunition.

Secret Mission in Nicosia

"Tonight, be ready to drive to Nicosia. We have orders to pick up weapons," Tryfonides said to me one afternoon. It was almost midnight when my aging Ford Prefect with the license 4546 arrived in Nicosia.

"Park here," Tryfonides told me. "We'll meet our contact in the cabaret on that corner." It was a well-known cabaret, Siantekler.

"Χριστός και Παναγία" (Christ and my Lady), Christakis," I said. "I never set foot in a cabaret, and you want me to go

---

[14]https://www.mixanitouxronou.com.cy/categories/istoria/ i-thriliki-apodrasitis-eoka-apo-tis-filakes-tis-kerinias- se-16-lepta-pos-kataferan-na-xegelasountous-anglous- desmofilakes/ [after opening the hyperlink click on the text then right click right click to translate into English]

now? You go!" I insisted. "I'll wait for you here. And can I ask you something? Is it through the cabarets that we are going to gain our liberation? I quit."

"What happened to you?" Christakis replied, "You can't disobey orders from the organization. You are a member of an underground organization, and you do not rule yourself. It's not your decision; it is the Chief's."

Very timidly, I descended the steps of the cabaret. We were greeted by a dancer named Corina. She was from Greece, and I confess that I was impressed by her beauty.

"Notis? He is not here," she said, "but he is going to be here any minute. He asked me to meet you." I confess I was very troubled by the ambiance.

Notis did not show up. By three in the morning, we were back in Limassol. The first thing that morning, I gave a detailed report to Andreas Ioannides, who was then the Leader of EOKA in Limassol.

He was a man of deep Christian and moral principles and was the Secretary of OXEN (Orthodox Christian Youth Association) of Limassol. He was so upset by what he heard that he immediately submitted his resignation. Digenis accepted it and placed Christakis Tryfonides as the Chief of the Limassol EOKA. Not so long after, Andreas Ioannidis was arrested by the English and held in detention at Kokkinotrimithia.

Notis, whose real name was Evagoras, came to Cyprus from Greece as a trainer. Very few of us had knowledge of the use of weapons and ammunition. We were all clueless about firearms and how to use them. On one occasion, we were informed that English soldiers had abandoned a suspicious device under a tree in the village of Ypsonas. A small group of us went to Ypsonas to find out what this was about.

"It's a high-powered mine," said our first guy.

"This is definitely an explosive object, and it will likely explode at any moment," said Fotis Iakovides.

All terrified, we laid on the ground, hiding behind a tree… and we left without knowing what this dangerous object was all about.

The next day, Digenis sent us Evagoras. The EOKA weapons expert enlightened us. Notis laughingly informed us that it was nothing more than just an old-style cooking stove!

Such was the military readiness of the Greek Cypriots in their war against the British Empire!

THE ETHOS OF DIGENIS

After the end of the Struggle, I learned that Digenis had similar complaints against Notis and ordered him to be executed. "I will not tolerate members to have relations with concubines and use the Organization for "scandalous purposes.""

After the intervention of Papastavrou, Notis's execution was aborted, and he was allowed to return to Greece. In matters of ethics, Digenis was tough and did not hesitate to punish severely, including even the organization's leaders, for improper conduct in homes that gave them cover.

In the book of Nikos Papanastasiou, "Lambros Kaykalidis: 'The Mouflon of EOKA'", he describes an incident that he observed firsthand and demonstrates the ethos of Digenis. Lambros Kaykalidis, a man with deeply rooted Christian virtues, who was close to Digenis as a member of the rebel group, described Digenis' reaction when members of the group asked permission to steal animals from a Turkish pen for a barbeque. In a grumpy style, he warned them:

"Goat thieves I have here? If you want a barbeque, ask, and I will give you money to buy it. I want you to be honest, not thieves." Lambros continues his description of Digenis:

"At every opportunity in writing, and orally, Digenis demanded that the EOKA members be honest in all aspects of their activity, especially well behaved in the homes giving them cover and when working with girls on joint missions. The punishment for all in case of disobedience of the order was one: death!"

Unfortunately, when Digenis had already died, EOKA B members[15] considered the looting of Turkish property an act of heroism and national duty!

When I got to know Digenis during the three months he stayed at our home, I found him to be a man of principle, strict, disciplined, and rich in his spiritual world. Unfortunately, in the sorrowful years of the national schism that followed, people who had been close to him did not hesitate to steal and pillage Turkish Cypriot property and do worse criminal acts. What is shameful is that such behavior was considered patriotic acts of heroism. What immoral decline from the years of the united Cypriot Hellenism and the heroic sacrifices embraced by the idealism of EOKA! Even more disturbing is that people who carried out such acts have remained unpunished, though they were largely responsible for the tragic course of our national problem.

---

[15] https://en.wikipedia.org/wiki/EOKA_B

On the Birthday of Queen Elizabeth

At the beginning of June 1955, I got an invitation from the British governor of Limassol for the birthday party of Queen Elizabeth. I went to the reception, but I left shortly before midnight because we had been ordered to blow up the Limassol Military Police Headquarters located close to the seafront. As planned, just before midnight, I passed by the clinic of Mario's Tritoftides, which was located east of the Public Garden on Byron Street, to pick up Bouboulina[16] to ride with us in the car for cover. Her real name was Aspasia. Bouboulina was her alias; she was a nurse working at the Tritoftides clinic.

Everyone in my house was asleep. Koyllapis had removed the explosive device from our crypt and waited for us in the darkness, hidden behind the banana bushes. Upon arriving at the Police Headquarters, Koyllapis swiftly placed the bomb in the Military Police Building's stairwell with the timer mechanism set to detonate at midnight.

Later, as I laid in bed, I could not sleep. I was constantly staring at the wall clock.

At midnight, a terrible explosion shook Limassol. Despite the objections and exhortations of Maroulla, I persuaded her to go along with me to personally see the extent of the damage caused by the explosion. Reporters were gathered at the scene, and many police officers were taking statements. Major damage was caused, with two military motorcycles destroyed.

Two years later, I found myself in the interrogation at Omorphita, and, among other things, I had to justify my presence outside the military police building after the explosion. It was not difficult for me. "I was leaving the

[16] https://en.wikipedia.org/wiki/Laskarina_Bouboulina

celebration of Her Majesty's Birthday, and when I heard the explosion, I came by to see what was going on."

ARREST OF TRYFONIDES
HADJIMILTIS- NEW LEADER IN LIMASSOL

A few days later, a crisis was created with the arrest of Tryfonides based on the newly enacted law on arrest and imprisonment without trial. He was taken to the Pyla Detention Center. Limassol was left without a chief. The new Limassol EOKA Chief appointed was Demos Hadjimiltis. He called us urgently to meet in his small room near the Metropolis Offices next to the church, known as Katholieke, to discuss the reorganization of the Limassol EOKA. We were Demos, Manolis Savvides, Andreas Morfitis, Andreas Papadopoulos, and Evgenios Kotsapas. We knew each other as friends who, besides our participation in EOKA, were active participants in OXEN's activities. Demos thought himself unfit to take on his great responsibility with the humility that characterized him. After much discussion, we ended up entrusting the administration of the Limassol EOKA to three people. Demos was to take over ambushes and bombing operations, Manolis Savvides, the Youth section, and I was to coordinate with other units and auxiliary services. Andonis Georgiadis told me later that Digenis laughed when he read Demos's report, who had the nickname "Lucifer," explaining our organization. Twisting his mustache, he said, "It seems it is Scouts we are organizing or Sunday School?"

My new duties

In the months that followed, my duties at the organization focused on the receipt, storage, and distribution of weapons and ammunition, all on orders from Hadjimiltis, the Limassol EOKA Chief. Also, I helped with the concealment of wanted persons, information gathering, mail handling, and the provision of various small tasks and services.

A serious problem in the availability of weaponry was created when the schooner Agios Georgios was intercepted by the British on the evening of 25 January 1955, at the location of "Rodafina", on Chloraka beach, north of Paphos, and new ways for access to weapons had to be established.

Members of the Organization stole from mines where they worked, supplied us with dynamite, slow-burning wicks, and detonators. When the importation of weapons from Greece was later organized through the Limassol Customs Team, many weapons were kept in our farm's crypt until instructions were given for their distribution. Our home and farm underwent many extensive searches expecting to find weapons, without success.

Makarios approval to purchase weapons

On a hot day in June 1955, sisters Nina and Lefki befriended an English soldier with their hospitality, offering him a cool soft drink. The Englishman, who was not so impressed by the drink as by the two charming sisters, returned to the girls' home several times. Once in a moment between serious and funny, Nina asked him if he could sell us revolvers. He agreed, asking for 25 pounds each. We thought we would take a chance. The next day we were entering the Archbishopric in Nicosia to consult with Makarios, who welcomed us warmly. After the serving of the typical Cyprus coffee, we got to the point. Makarios listened carefully to Demos about the Englishman's offer. He (Makarios) wanted to know what we knew about revolvers. Truly little, of course. We could identify the cylindrical from the flat ones and learn about the various calibers, and not much more.

It looked as if Makarios was surprised at our ignorance and perhaps wondering how people like us, clueless about weapons and guns, could cope with the mighty British Empire. At one point, he opened his desk drawer, pulled out a big revolver, and put it in front of us. "That's a 38- caliber Colt," he said. "If you can find such, you have my approval to purchase as many as you can." We left, and as I was walking down the steps of the Archdiocese satisfied, I was tempted to whisper in Demos' ear, the Cypriot saying: "Rather than a murdered priest, better a priest who is…". I did not dare complete this popular proverb.[17]

The beloved Hadjimiltis, in his book "The Braves of 55" (p. 40), describes how the first lessons in the handling of an automatic weapon were provided to us by an English soldier.

During one of the authorities' frequent curfews, we found ourselves confined in the home of Savvas and Kyriaki Drousiotis on busy Agia Zone Street in Limassol. The couple's two daughters, Nina (later wife of Hadjimiltis) and Lefki Drousiotis, as members of EOKA, offered valuable services to the Liberation Struggle.

The English soldiers were in and out

---

[17] "Instead of a killed priest, it is better for the priest to be the killer!"

of the house looking for weapons. While gladly accepting Cypriot hospitality and the girls' company, they looked for wanted men, departing confident of performing their duty. On one occasion, one of the soldiers noticed that we were curiously looking at his automatic.

"Do you want to know how it works?" he asked the two of us.

The Englishman took our inquiry seriously and spent a long time explaining how an automatic weapon worked and what we had to look out for our safety in its use. We listened with awe and unabated attention to the English soldier's instructions who, before saying goodbye to us with his thanks for the hospitality we had offered, "reassured" us that it was only a matter of time for the 40,000 British soldiers to arrest Digenis and crush EOKA!

MISLEADING INFORMATION

Few days passed before we received information that near the monastery of Panagia Sfalagiotisas, there was a crypt with a large number of weapons. It filled us with great joy. According to the information, the weapons were buried under a tree located 125 meters east of the church's sanctuary. Demos commissioned me to find the hidden treasure. I called Christakis Antoniou, known as Kitsios, and Sofoklis Potamitis, and we left for Sfalagiotisas. Christakis was a member of the Omodos team, known for his daring, determination, and patriotism. Sophocles also did not lack in his commitment to our liberation struggle, and he also had technical knowledge about weapons and ammunition. We went to Sfalantiotissa on a tractor, carrying various agricultural tools to have an alibi, in case we were stopped by the British.

We dug around for three days with many precautions hoping that we would find the hidden weapons. It turned out that we did not find anything, and Demos ordered us to stop the search. We were concerned about the source and motive behind this misleading information. Gregory Afxentiou later answered. The story had been invented by Petros Hadjimiltis, a member of his team in Pentadaktylos.

Petros Hadjimiltis, who had nothing to do with EOKA, was sentenced to many years of imprisonment for murder. In prison, he became acquainted with EOKA fighters whom he convinced of his supposedly pure patriotic sentiments. He left the prison in an escape, staged by the English, joining Gregory Afxentiou in Kythrea, who oversaw the EOKA operations of the Pentadaktikos mountain range at the time. Digenis, acquainted with Hadjimiltis' criminal past, ordered his execution. But Afxentiou, instead of carrying out the order, decided to test Hadjimiltis by assigning him to execute an informant in Kythrea. Instead of carrying out this mission, Hadjimiltis went to the police and gave a detailed description of the movements of Afxentiou and his team. The consequence of this betrayal was an extensive British operation in Pentadaktylos from 31 October to 6 November, in which the informant participated undercover. Afxentiou and his team were ultimately rescued because Putty Stokos, an officer of the Police Special Branch and a member of EOKA, was listening through the wall when a Greek Cypriot policeman translated the informant's testimony to British officers. The case did not stop there. Afxentiou was ordered to meet with Digenis, who then had his headquarters in Spilia in the Troodos mountain range.

DIGENIS ORDERS AFXENDIU TO MEET AT SPILIA

The meeting of Gregory Afxentiou[18] with his leader, Digenis, in Spilia on 29 November 1955, is vividly described by the writer and researcher Leonidas Leonidou in his book "George Grivas Digenis", vol. II, page 226

> *Afxentiou saluted Digenis, according to military etiquette. Digenis, in austere style: "Who are you to disobey my orders?" Mr. Afxentiou, standing still: "At your command, Chief!".*

Afxentiou's stay in Spilia proved to be a lifesaver for Digenis and the Organization. By 11 December, the English had surrounded the forest in which Digenis was with his team. When they were at imminent risk of being discovered by the English, Afxentiou, with a clever military maneuver - and completely alone, managed to fire his automatic rifle, creating sufficient confusion among the English, to allow Digenis and his team to escape safely to Kakopetria.

A DANGEROUS MEETING

In May 1956, Manolis Savvides, a close family friend and in charge of the Youth Sector of EOKA in Limassol, told me that an English informant was watching me and briefing the police on my movements. The house of a Greek Cypriot officer in charge of the Crime Detection Department was then located directly opposite Manolis's house.

---

[18] https://en.wikipedia.org/wiki/Grigoris_Afxentiou

"I suggest," said Manolis, "to risk it and speak openly to the Greek Cypriot officer and to ask him to join the organization and become our informant. But because this would be a dangerous mission for him, tell him that if he betrayed you, think about the consequences that he and his family could have." He had a daughter he loved.

We got approval from our Chief, and so I visited the Greek Cypriot officer at his house. I asked for the two of us to meet alone. He brought me coffee, and I got right to the point.

"You have three choices, I said: 1) betray me and suffer the consequences, 2) join the organization and contribute to the fight for the liberation of Cyprus, or 3) withdraw and not come after us".

He remained silent for a few minutes. I did not talk either; the atmosphere was heavy. When he broke the silence, he said, "I can't join the organization, but I promise I won't participate in any action that turns against you."

Manolis watched from his home window, anxious to see what would happen. If a police car would come to arrest me, would I get out of the house unharmed?

I valued the honesty of my police officer, who also kept his promise. His conduct contributed to his promotion in the ranks of the police corps when Cyprus gained its independence.

When I was arrested and interrogated at Omorphita, my inquisitor named the informant who reported to the Greek Cypriot officer, saying that I had a role in a plan with EOKA to kidnap him. While this Officer was aware of the abduction plan, he did not mention anything to the English interrogators against me.

AN AMBUSH DESIGNED WITH... PAPOUTSOSIKA! (FRANGKOSYKA)

In mid-August 1955, I was instructed to deliver an automatic rifle and a grenade to the Kalo Chorio Village EOKA team. I was born in Kalo Chorio and had close links and relationships. However, due to the underground structure and the organization's revolutionary character, members were forced to remain anonymous and not reveal secrets to third parties, even close relatives. Because my home was used as a cache of weapons and ammunition distributed island wide, I was exposed to a wide circle of my fellow fighters. With the group of Kalo Chorio, I had closer ties and, although the team was under the command of Afxentiou, I remained in close contact.

We met one night in the village to discuss the details of an ambush. We chose a location near the "sweet water" between Gerasa and Kalo Chorio. It was a dirt road with a steep turn on which large cars could not get through without maneuvering and changing gears 2-3 times back and forth. We considered it an ideal location for the ambush. But how could an ambush be set up with only one automatic rifle and a grenade? There were six members on the team, and they all wanted to take part. But apart from a few detonators and a few meters of wick, we could not spare any more weapons.

Then Faidros Elias reassured us. "I've got a solution!"

The hills are loaded with cactus. We will fill up two baskets of cactus fruit, and when the military jeeps reach the bend, we will shower them with the spiny cactus fruit. We laughed our hearts out but felt relieved. "Let's try it," we said.

The team waited all night, but hours later, still, no British car had come by, so we could not ascertain our new weapon's effectiveness! Inexperienced, unarmed, and often naïve, with only the weapons of our faith and enthusiasm in the pro-freedom struggle, we were not aware that we were facing the British lion before us.

THE DANGER OF BEING ARRESTED IN AGRIDA

We were at the house of Elias Balanidi, at the village of Agridia, when close by, we heard the Greek national anthem being sung. "Elias, please go and tell them to stop singing. We'll all be arrested," I said. He went to tell them to stop right now. When he came back, he told me, "Boss, they slaughtered the pig. It weighed 400 okes (1 oke = 2.8 lbs.), and from their excitement, they're singing the national anthem"![19] The national sentiment and desire for Union touched all aspects of human existence.

"FREE CYPRUS RADIO STATION"

A few days after he took command, Demos Hadjimiltis became the Chief of EOKA in Limassol. I was informed that Totos Pilavakis offered to install a radio station for the Organization. Totos maintained a laboratory of electronic devices in Limassol and had a reputation as a specialist in loudspeaker installations, radio repairs, and other electronic devices.

We were fascinated by the idea that we could respond to RIK (the Cyprus Government Radio), the British propaganda instrument. Totos installed a transmitter at our farm and adjusted the wavelength to be close to the British radio station's frequency.

When the radio transmitter was ready, we decided to

---

[19] https://en.wikipedia.org/wiki/Hymn_to_Liberty

do the first test. Demos was to make the test presentation. Eugene Kotsapas and I were waiting in a car to hear and judge the transmission quality. We parked close to the button factory and turned on the radio, waiting anxiously to listen to Demos. Soon we heard him say, "I am speaking to you from the monastery of Troditissas, from the Abbot's office." We both burst out laughing, both because of our enthusiasm for the radio station's success and by the humor of Demos. He called our house "the monastery" because not a day would pass without having visitors and fighters from distant areas, and many times Turkish Cypriots as our guests. It was customary to invite all to eat with us and occasionally spend the night.

However, it was not long before our enthusiasm turned into disappointment. A member of the organization who worked with the Government's radio station's technical crew informed us that our transmission was recorded. The English would locate the transmitter by some electronic means. A helicopter taking off from the Akrotiri British base, making circles over Limassol, could identify the broadcast source. So (unfortunately), the radio station idea did not go ahead.

Informing the public was entrusted to PEKA, the Cyprus Struggle's Political Committee, mainly by distributing leaflets and notices.[20] An important contribution was also

[20] The PEKA was founded in 1956, and the goals and objectives established by order of the military leader of the race-Georgios Grivas Digenis, dated 03.09.1956. PEKA was founded by Georgios Grivas and was independent of EOKA (= National Organization of Cypriot Fighters) and ANE (= Alkimos Youth EOKA). However, PEKA acted in parallel and assisted the work of EOKA, which was a purely military organization.
http://www.polignosi.com/cgibin/hweb?-A=8964&-V=limmata

made by the Alkimos youth organization founded by EOKA in mid-1957.[21]

KOSTAS EFSTATHIOU, FAT-KOSTAS

Kostas Efstathiou was a high-ranking officer of the Cypriot police, known throughout Cyprus for his honesty, patriotism, and profound Christian faith. Because of his very imposing physical dimensions, he was known as Pachi (Fat) Kostas.

He had come to my office a few months previously and asked to see me in private. I was worried for a moment. As the colonial government forces were known, members of the "security forces" have always caused some fear. Digenis' instructions were clear. "Do not trust anyone."

Kostas put his hand on my shoulder and lowered his voice, whispered into my ear.

"I want you to swear my whole family and me into the EOKA." He lived with his wife, Agnes, and their children: Eustace, Spyros, and Maria, in a small orchard near the Germasogeia River.

"Mr. Efstathiou," I replied, using a serious tone, "I have no idea. I have no contact with EOKA, nor do I interfere in such cases."

"You are not the son of Papasolomou? Think!!! What did I ask of you? We will talk again," was his answer.

He smiled and finished his coffee and stood up to leave

I contacted Demos immediately. All our information about Pachi Kostas was positive both in town as well as in
[21]http://www.polignosi.com/cgibin/hweb?-A=1278&-V=limmata

the countryside. He enjoyed high esteem and was known as a man of principle, committed to his family and work.

From his Senior Police position, he could give us valuable information and cover for dangerous missions. That same afternoon I called Pachi Kostas' phone number. "When you get a chance, I would like to see you."

A few minutes later, he arrived in the little red Hillman he was driving. His face shined with pleasure when I informed him of the decision. "Get in the car now," Pachi Kostas said. "Let us go to my home."

Mrs. Agnes was a kind, cheerful, hospitable, and very hard-working woman. She welcomed me with a lot of goodwill. She brought us cherry cake and coffee and invited me to stay with them for dinner.

"Bring the icons here," Pachi Kostas' told her. "Bring the kids." I objected to the children coming. But he insisted. "I want the whole family to join. Don't worry. I'm my family's boss," he said.

In no time, all of them knelt, and Pachi Kostas read the

Oath of the Organization.[22] He was now a member of EOKA and remained in close contact with me. This brought us almost daily information on the army's movements and the police and any informants in the police ranks, and he undertook the transportation of suspects and weapons. He was always willing to help.

When Digenis later lived in our house, he ordered me to put a hole in the warehouse's wooden wall where he spent most of the day with Adonis Georgiadis to watch and listen to what was going on outside.

"Listen," he told me one morning. "When Pachi Kostas comes, bring him around so I can overhear his conversations." Pachi Kostas was very descriptive in discussions, enriching the stories and anecdotes from his life in the police force. For Digenis, the visits of Pachi Kostas were the real entertainment. Impressed by his great dimensions, one time, in a humorous mood, he asked me, "Did you ask him to tell you how he makes love to his wife?"

---

[22] EOKA OATH: I swear in the name of the Holy Trinity that: I shall work with all my power for the liberation of Cyprus from the British yoke sacrificing for this even my life; I shall perform without objection all the instructions of the organization which may be entrusted to me and I shall not bring any objection, however difficult and dangerous these may be; I shall not abandon the struggle unless I receive instructions from the leader of the organization and after our aim has been accomplished; I shall never reveal to anyone any secret of our organization neither the names of my chiefs nor those of the other members of the organization even if I am caught and tortured; I shall not reveal any of the instructions, which may be given me even to my fellow combatants. If I disobey my oath, I shall be worthy of every punishment as a traitor and may eternal contempt cover me.

THE DANGEROUS METAPHOR OF PRIAMOS

"Priamos" was the alias of Lefkios Rodosthenous, who was wanted by the authorities, with a 5,000-pound reward for information leading to his arrest. He was Chief of the EOKA section of the West Limassol region, with his headquarters in Prastio Avdimou village.

Pachi Kostas arrived one night at my house late. He seemed anxious. It would have been already past ten. He was talking breathlessly. "At midnight," he said, "I have information that the security forces will surround Prastio."

I immediately informed Demos and drove to meet Lefkios to take him away from Prastio. It was midnight when I picked him up to bring him to Limassol. As we left, we could hear of the military convoy arriving with their vehicle lights turned off.

There was no bypass road like today of the Akrotiri British base at that time, so we had to drive through it.

We agreed with Lefkios for me to talk in case we were stopped for questioning as to our whereabouts. He had a fake ID with him that presented him as a worker in the British bases.

Outside of Paramali, we were stopped at the first roadblock. "What are you doing here, and where have you come from at this late hour?" "We were in Pissouri. We went to serve a customer, and we remained for some fun."

"What about your passenger?" "He does not speak English; he is a worker at the British bases in Akrotiri, as you can confirm from his ID."

The officer seemed satisfied with our explanations, but he also proceeded to do a thorough examination of the car.

They had us get out of the car to do a rigorous search for documents and weapons. In the end, they lifted the car to investigate from below. The two of us were watching in silence. We sighed with relief when the officer in charge told us we could leave.

By the time we got to Limassol, we had gone through two more checks without anything incriminating the two of us. "God saved us, as the mission of the newly appointed Governor of Cyprus, Field Marshal Harding, was to crush EOKA, and one of his first actions was to impose the death penalty for anyone found with weapons or hiding 'the wanted'."

DIGENIS IS SETTLES IN LIMASSOL

In June 1956, the news came that the English had set fire to the Paphos forest to burn Digenis and his team alive; this news shook us. But Digenis escaped in the nick of time by breaking through, fleeing to Saitas and on to Gerasa village in a dramatic escape of skill and luck, eluding his arrest. Demos came hurriedly to my home to see me. Nina Drousiotis was with him. She offered invaluable services to Chief Digenis personally and the Organization in general.

"We urgently need to transfer the weapons elsewhere and prepare the hideout because the Chief wants to come to Limassol." He told me about the meeting he had in Gerasa where, in addition to Digenis, were Andonis Georgiadis, Lefkios Rodosthenous, and Gregory Afxentiou. Afxentiou was trying to persuade Digenis to move towards Zoopiyi and then eastward to the Makhairas forest. Along the way, all the villages had strong EOKA teams and he would be safe in this route. Digenis, with his characteristic insightful intuition, however, preferred to move closer to Limassol.

"Demos," I said, "it would be a great honor for us to be able to host the Chief at our home in Limassol, but the whole of Cyprus knows me. He wouldn't be safe, and we would be taking on immense responsibility."

"Indeed," said Demos, "the first thing Digenis asked me was to tell him how many know that Adonis (which was my nickname) is a member of the Organization." I told him, "2-3, at most, four people, Chief." "Dafnis, we have no better option than your place. We'll risk it temporarily until we find a better and safer place to install the Chief of our Organization and its headquarters."

"And watch out, Adonis," Demos said strictly. "If he asks you the same questions, give the same answer. He'll execute us both on the spot if he realizes we're lying!"

I heard him in awe. "Well," I said, "May God's will be done."

We laughed hilariously at our problem-solving skills, where our choices were playing "heads or tails" with our lives and the future of the Cyprus liberation struggle!

Demos instructed me to arrange a meeting with our member, the police officer, Kostas Efstathiou. In the late afternoon of 18 June, Demos informed Pachi Kostas that they would be traveling somewhere together to transport a trainer of the organization to my house that night.

"You'll be the driver, and you must keep quiet, not opening your mouth to say anything. You will not even turn your head to see them."

Pachi Kostas asked to have his wife, Mrs. Agnes, come

along, to which Demos gave his consent.

Digenis' relocation to Limassol was a dangerous seminal mission of immense importance to the Cyprus Liberation Struggle's future. Demos, in his book "The Braves Ones of 1955", describes the event as follows:

> *"Early in the morning of the next day, I visited Daphne Panagides to inform him that he would temporarily host Digenis in the hideout he had built under his garage. I told him of my meeting with the Chief and explained to Daphne the reasons for the move of Digenis to our city. I urged the utmost discretion from him and his family members. We agreed on the great responsibility that we were now assuming for the future of the Struggle and its Leader, Digenis. He accepted the news with deep emotion. He did not show the slightest hesitation. The same emotion of welcome and pride was shown by all the family members when I announced the big news to his wife, Maroulla, and his brother, Stahis. The passage of time would confirm the wisdom of the choice of the Panagides family to host Digenis."*

Demos delineated the plan for the transfer of Digenis from Gerasa, where he had arrived following his escape from the British encirclement in Troodos and his assistant Andonis Georgiades, Lefkios Rodosthenous, and the guerrilla fighter, Lambros Kaykalidis.

For security reasons, in case there would be a military

roadblock, a car preceded Pachi Kostas, driven by Andreas Papadopoulos with passengers - my brother, Stahis, who was the leader of the EOKA Youth Organization at the Lanition Gymnasium of Limassol, his fiancée, Elena Lamari, and Elizabeth Nicolaou. Pachi Kostas's car followed behind with passengers: his wife, Agni, Digenis, Andonis Georgiadis, Demos Hadjimiltis, and Nina Drousiotis.

Demos continued in the same book that we mentioned above:

> *"I had the feeling that the road would never end. The one and a half hours that it took to arrive at our destination seemed like a year. During the entire trip, no one in the car uttered a single word. Upon arriving outside the house of Dafnis Panagides, the agony was replaced with relief ... the Panagides family reception by Dafnis, his wife, Maroulla, and his brother Stahis, was warm and moving. You saw it in everyone's faces, the admiration and deep concern. I personally felt satisfied with choosing the Panagides family home to welcome our leader with hospitality in an environment of absolute trust and security."*

When Pachi Kostas learned, at the end of the struggle (1959), that he had transferred Digenis in his car, he hurried to Athens to meet him. Digenis hugged him and kissed him, and they conversed for quite a while.

"What's your impression of Digenis, Kostas?" I asked him when he returned.

"I will never forgive you for not telling me when I was transporting Digenis, to be more careful. But I enjoyed his kalamaristiki (Athenian) accent, pronouncing my name Paxi Kostas, with a soft 'sh,' instead of the Cypriot 'Pachi Kostas'."

THE ARRIVAL OF DIGENIS AT OUR HOME

Our agony had peaked when the clock struck midnight, and neither Digenis nor Andonis Georgiadis had yet been seen. Finally, a few minutes before one, the 19th of June 1956, our agony had reached the highest; we welcomed Digenis and Andonis Georgiades to our home. It was the first time I met Digenis, the legend of the Cyprus struggle for freedom. He was a real person that we could touch and admire, the embodiment of heroism, self- sacrifice, and self-denial. His big eyebrows and characteristic piercing stare touched my heart. My wife Maroulla and I, following the traditional Cypriot gesture for respect, kissed his hand.

"Chief," I said, "We were worried when you were late."

"The Virgin Mary has saved us, but just, so you know, neither God nor Mary protect fools." And he went on: "How many (people) know that you are a member of the Organization and how many about your home?"

As agreed with Demos to hide the truth, since if we said that our house was a center of fugitives and temporary storage of weapons, the Chief would have refused to stay, and then we would face a huge problem hiding him.

"Two-three people of trust, Chief," was my answer.

"Up to three? That is good. Otherwise, we are not safe."

My wife, Maroulla, after offering him fresh lemonade, asked him what he preferred for tomorrow's meal. He answered right away: "Plenty of fruit, garlic, mustard, legumes, and vegetables."

So began his stay at our house that lasted until September 14 when the Chief moved to his new hideout in the lot adjacent to our orchard, which had been rented by the organization from the owner Hambis Demetriou.

In the three months that Digenis stayed with us, we shared moments of pleasure and moments of agony, moments mixed with feelings of joy and sorrow, depending on the news that we waited anxiously to hear from the radio and the EOKA regional Chiefs.

We waited anxiously every day for Nina Drousiotis to correspond with the Regional Chiefs and bring us reports from all over Cyprus. He read them and, depending on the content, his face revealed his reaction.

In one case, he burst into laughter. "Come and see what she writes." He was talking about the report from the Larnaca Chief, Elenitsa Seraphim. She reported that the youth groups' glue to stick leaflets on the walls was not working, and she was asking Digenis for instructions on how to make a more powerful glue.

"Ha, ha, ha," he said, rubbing his mustache. "Soon, they'll ask me how to have children!"

His daily exercise was necessary. In the evenings, he enjoyed short walks under cover of the orchard's lemon trees. When he was not engaged with the Organization business, he liked to work on his stamp collection.

He was especially careful with his diet. He did not smoke or drink; he was mostly vegetarian and rarely ate meat. He shaved daily, paying a lot of attention to his mustache.

We enjoyed our walk with him, telling us stories about his military campaigns in Asia Minor and Pindos[23][24]. The Greek force had reached only 25 kilometers from the Turkish capital, Ankara, and waited for instructions for their next move when they brought him a Turkish mother with three children. She was terrified, begging him not to hurt her. Instead, the Greek soldiers offered her food and medical treatment and then let her go. In tears, she kneeled before Grivas and kissed his feet.

He was also known for his humanity when, after capturing a young English soldier in an ambush at Chandria, the team wanted to execute the prisoner. "No," he told them rigorously, "He has a mother just like you do. He is a prisoner of war."

As I got to know Digenis during the three months he stayed with us, I found him very humane, humorous, modest, and accessible. His patriotism and disciplined commitment, and devotion to the struggle were an inspiration and source of strength for us all.

HOW THE ENGLISH PERCEIVED DIGENS

Understanding the personality of Digenis had occupied the British Secret Service.

Documents of the British M16 Security Intelligence Service, which were declassified in 2014, revealed their attempt to describe General Grivas' obsessions. The aim was to find evidence from his anti-communist actions by

---

[23]https://en.wikipedia.org/wiki/Greco-Turkish_War_ (1919%E2%80%931922)
[24]https://en.wikipedia.org/wiki/Greek_Civil_War

his Organization "X"[25] during the Greek Civil war, to incite confrontation with the Cypriot left. The M16 document described General Grivas as a "good professional and courageous soldier, a fan of the monarchy and 'a Fierce Anticommunist'."

The interest of the English in Digenis continued after the signing of the Zurich London-Agreements. On 3 November 1959, Brigadier General Bill McGann, the Director of M15, attempted to outline General Grivas' personality. McGann described Digenis as an unusual man, who was not of abstract theory but a man of practicality, a man of principle, but who at the same time had no qualms in deciding to kill someone though without a trace of sadism. Of course, the document also listed negative characteristics describing General Grivas as an irritable opportunist without insight.

Ironically, half a century after his death, the EOKA struggle is part of the curriculum, plus lessons learned at the British Royal Military Academy. Each year a group of the Academy students, the future leaders of the British Forces, visits the Digenis Hideout in Limassol, as well as the Struggle Museum in Nicosia to learn about Digenis and EOKA and how and why one of Britain's most experienced Marshals (Harding) with more than 40,000 English soldiers could not defeat (them) in a small area such as the Island of Cyprus.

THE ENGLISH DISCOVER THE DIARY OF DIGENS AFTER TREASON.

At the beginning of August 1956, the British authorities announced that they had discovered the personal diary of Digenis and began to selectively publish some of its contents. In many cases, the British also modified some of his writings

[25] https://en.wikipedia.org/wiki/Organization_X

and printed them to undermine his prestige, create division in the Fighters' ranks, and the relations among Makarios, Digenis, and Athens.

Digenis' dismay was obvious when the diary was discovered and was misused. For days, he stayed quiet, introspective, not wanting to eat anything.

DIGENIS RECOMMENDS THE CREATION OF AN "AXIS"

Digenis' communication with Archbishop Makarios and Athens was continuous. During one of our evening walks, he seemed anxious. I dared to ask him if he had any problems with his health. He was upset by a letter he had received from Athens informing him of the Greek Government's rejection of his recommendation for creating an "axis" with Yugoslavia, Greece, and Egypt's participation. For Digenis, such an alliance axis would allow Greece to play a decisive role in geopolitical developments in the Middle East with favorable outcomes for Cyprus's struggle for union with Greece. But the Greek foreign policy, clearly defined by NATO, had no such policy options.

THE GREAT SEARCH FOR OUR HOUSE

I was at the village of Lyssi when a phone call from the late Thanos Ellinas, a close family friend, made me freeze. "Your house," he told me, "is surrounded by dozens of English soldiers and Turkish auxiliary police, perhaps as many as three hundred. Do not return to Limassol until we see what happens."

THE HOUSE AT KALO CHORIO LIMASSOL WHERE DAFNIS WAS BORN

Black thoughts flooded my mind. Betrayed, I thought. There goes the struggle for Cyprus independence; it is all gone!

Together with my koumbaros (best man) Vasilis Koysiappas, we kneeled and prayed while his wife offered incense to the Holy Icons. I at once left Lyssi to get closer to Limassol. I do not recall how I could have driven to Lefkara. I contacted our liaison there and got Thanos Ellinas on the phone. "The investigation continues," he said. I replied, "They won't find anything, and they will be disappointed. I have nothing to do with EOKA." I thought to say this assuming that my phone was being tapped, but the feeling of agony was great inside me.

"The searching continues, and they're digging with spades in the fields, and they also have dogs," he replied.

It began to get dark, and my hopes started to rise. I tried calling again, but I could not get a line. We anxiously turned on the radio, and we heard, "The security forces conducted a large-scale search on a farm near Limassol." With no more news, I was assured that the search was unsuccessful. General Grivas, Adonis Georgiadis, and well, my entire family were safe. "Thank you, oh God," I said, and I started for Limassol.

Maroulla was full of emotion and hugged me and kissed me. "A miracle saved us," she said, describing the search in detail. The soldiers and auxiliary police surrounded our house early in the morning. As I found out from the interrogations that I later underwent at Omorphita, the investigations were based on information that we were hiding weapons on the farm, which was true. The search focused on finding the weaponry, not Grivas. They had dug up our orchard inch by Inch. On her knees in the room, Maroulla prayed intensively; she was a woman of deep faith. I had a lot of personal experiences, which showed that her prayers had had a direct response. In one moment during the search, a Turkish auxiliary policeman spotted a partially buried electrical cord. It was the power cord that gave the hideout its light and ventilation fan. He began to dig it up, pulled slowly, and approached the shelter where Grivas and Adonis Georgiadis were hiding.

Maroulla's breathing had stopped, but she did not stop praying. The policeman following the cable was only 2-3 meters from the hideout entrance. At that moment, our unforgettable mother, Maria Solomon Panagides "Konomissa" (as everyone called her), was watching from the kitchen window as the Turk was pulling up the cable. In a moment of determination and courage, she bolted out of the kitchen and grabbed the Turk auxiliary by his jacket as if to protect him, yelling at him loudly, "Son, you're ruining our lights, and the power will burn you!" At that time, the English officer-in-charge of the operation's whistle was heard, followed by the command: "The Search Is Over!". Nothing less of a miracle was the failure of the search to discover Grivas. If the search succeeded, the consequences would have been dramatic with the collapse of the Cyprus Independent struggle with my hanging and likely execution of my brother.

MOVING DIGENIS TO A NEW HIDEOUT

Not much time had passed when Digenis became aware that my house was a busy place. Not only did fellow fighters come by to discuss issues of the Organization, but also my clients from all over Cyprus, and including many Turkish Cypriots. In one case, we hosted the Chief of the Larnaca EOKA, Elenitsa Seraphim-Loizou. When we sat for dinner, she noticed two extra plates and asked if we should wait for these other guests.

In her book *The Liberation Struggle of Cyprus 1955-1959*, Elenitsa says that she suspected we were hiding fugitives. Still, she could not have imagined that just a few meters from where she was sitting, Digenis himself was hiding.

Digenis began to feel apprehensive and decided it would be better to move to a new hideout. He instructed me to rent the adjacent farm where the isolated farmhouse was located, under the pretext that an uncle of mine who lived in Africa was coming to Cyprus to plant clover. Mr. Hambis, the owner of the farm, signed the contract, but the three sisters (known for their beauty), who rented the place despite repeated pressures and exhortations on my part, were not going to move. They were engaged in the "women's profession" and were known as "the Tziaxoudes Sisters." They had a wide range of clients that included high-ranking civil servants, many Turks, and others.

We had to move the three sisters from the house to prepare the new hideout for Digenis as soon as possible. He would not accept an excuse for delay. After three postponements for the move, I came back one Saturday to tell him that, although I had found another home for the ladies and had paid the first month's rent, the three sisters did not keep their promise to move and remained in the rental because they would not bother my uncle and even that they could help with the housework. I walked timidly into the hideout, and even before finishing my sentence, I was slapped twice by Digenis, the heaviest blows I ever had in my life.

Enraged, he said to me, "You will betray us. Get out of here," and with a strong kick, he threw me out of the hideout.

For more than a month, when the sisters left the house, the new hideout construction got underway; I had no contact with Digenis. Only my beloved wife, Maroulla, communicated with him. After the intermediation of Andonis Georgiadis and after Nina Drousiotis convinced me that I was not in danger, I dared to go back to the hideout to visit him. He accepted me with hugs and joy.

"Well, where did you go and disappear for so long? From today, you will not leave Limassol. You will go to the cafes to hear what they say about EOKA and Digenis and share it with us at night." And indeed, I did that for a long time. We spent many nights laughing with the anecdotes circulated about Digenis, which he was waiting to hear.

"What did you hear today?" he would ask.

"Chief, why don't you tell us how the British greeted you at the Akrotiri base this morning?"

"Are you crazy?" he would respond.

"I was having my coffee at Sykaminia Café that day when I overheard a group at the next table talking about Digenis saying, 'Have you heard the latest news, George? Digenis visited the Akrotiri base yesterday disguised as an English officer and was received with honors.'"

Digenis burst out laughing!

When in November 1956, after I was locked in Pyla detention prison, Grivas told Marios and Ellie Christodoulides: "They took this one too [Dafnis], who with his stories made us laugh."

Finally, the three sisters left the premises. On the pretext that we were excavating for a septic tank, a small group of workers began constructing the new hideout. We have chosen fighters distinguished for their integrity of character and their devotion to the ideals of faith and Motherland Greece to help in the digging to prepare the hideout as soon as possible. They would start work when darkness fell and would leave before dawn.

Early in September, the new hideaway was finally ready. With relief, Digenis heard that he could move the next night.

But while everything was ready and the family of Marios Christodoulides had already moved to settle in, an unexpected obstacle occurred. The door to the hideout would not close!

"Chief," I say, "we have a problem with the trap door, and we need to delay your move for 24 hours," I explained to him that the concrete's moisture had caused the wooden door to expand, and it was impossible to close.

He listened to this with discomfort. "What's up? Why won't the door close? Who made the design?"

"The Pindos Chief! He is a graduate of the National Technical University of Athens."

"Tell him to X such a degree. I don't have a university degree, and all the hideouts I've designed have not been a problem."

He took a piece of paper and made a draft to modify the door.

When he was later informed that the English were pouring water on floors to make sure there was no camouflaged entrance to a hideout, he ordered a sponge to be fitted for greater safety, a very effective modification.

MARIOS AND ELLI CHRISTODOULIDES

We had already signed the contract to rent the farm next to our farm owned by Hambis Demetriou. I planted clover to breed cows and informed folks that one of my uncles was coming from Africa to manage the farm. This was told for the satisfaction of Mr. Hambis! But how about Digenis' safety?

Trying to find a family that could take on the house with its inordinate responsibility was not easy, and our searching for such a family lasted several weeks. We were looking for an unpretentious person, above all suspicion, and most of all, a person of absolute confidence and trust. The late and unforgettable Manolis Savvides found the solution.

"My colleague, Marios Christodoulides, is the right person for this if he accepts to do it," he informed us one night in a meeting with the Chief. Marios was a colleague of Manolis; they had both worked at the Ottoman bank. Marios had the Ottoman bank branch's responsibility at the Episkopi Station, which meant that he could enter the British bases.

Manolis informed Marios, who was living at Polemidia with his wife Elli, and children Soula and Myriam, about the need. The first sounding out was exploratory to determine whether Marios would accept a house in Limassol's suburbs.

What was wanted was someone to hide Greek officers who were in Cyprus, helping our liberation struggle. Marios was positive, provided that his wife Elli would accept.

The next day, Manolis and I met Marios under a tree outside Polemidia in a secluded area. It was then only fields. This was the first time I met Marios Christodoulides. He was thin, tall, and smiling. My first impression was positive. We proceeded to reveal to him that he would be taking on one of the most dangerous and the most serious missions of the liberation struggle: the safekeeping, the protection, and the care of Digenis himself! Marios sank into deep thoughts, not saying a word. He was moved at the great honor, but at the same time, he was fully aware of the dangers to which he was exposing himself and his family.

When everything was ready for the move, Digenis set a difficult condition. He did not want the couple's daughter, four years old, Soula, in the house. She would have to stay with her grandmother. But under what pretext? On what grounds can a mother leave her child in the hands of grandma and settle in the city? So Marios staged a scene with his mother-in-law, and in his "anger," he grabbed his wife and two other daughters and left Polemidia with a stern warning to his mother-in-law, "Don't you dare come around me!"

It is difficult to imagine the feelings that such behavior might have arisen in all the parties involved. Such sacrifice and commitment of mental power where the love of the homeland transcends the love of the children, as in this case, shows the immense contribution of the couple, Marios and Ellis Christodoulides, to the Cyprus liberation struggle. Months passed before Ellie revealed to her mother that their move to Limassol and their separation from their little daughter, Soula, was a necessary sacrifice "for serious national reasons."

"But my daughter?" was the proud reaction of the mother of Elli, "You are with EOKA, and you did not tell me?"

The problem was when the Reverend Papa Georgios, the priest at the near-by Saint Nicholas church, arrived to perform the traditional blessing for the newcomers, bearing incense and holy water. He was knocking at the door, but the hostess would not open it. He was sure there were people in the house - he kept hearing a baby crying.

He came to be concerned about the new residents' personality, saying, "But what kind of people came to our neighborhood, Daphne?"

"Confidentially, Father George, I must tell you that this is a woman who took the wrong path, and we recommended that the family separate from her to protect the family reputation. Father, do not bother because her husband is even jealous of priests." He made the sign of the cross and smiled. "As we get older, we see puzzling things…"

On the night of 14September, when darkness fell, Chief Digenis with Adonis Georgiadis moved to the new hideout that remained the Struggle headquarters until its end in February 1959.

THE ENGLISH WANT TO SEE ME!

Early October 1956, I was in Paphos when my wife, Maroulla, informed me that a group of English soldiers accompanied by a Turkish auxiliary came to the house and asked to "see" me. They left an order for me to contact the Red House upon my return to Limassol. Maroulla informed Digenis, who asked to see me as soon as I got back, taking every precaution as my movements would be monitored. That same afternoon, Digenis ordered me to report to the Red House posing as a law-abiding citizen. He ruled out the option of joining a rebel group, observing that "he would not kill even an ant."

"I'm not worried about the interrogations," he said, "watch your words and have my blessing."

In Grivas' diary, he writes:

> *"Among our arrested members ... were three who knew my place of residence and had constructed my hideout, Dafnis Panagides, Andreas Papadopoulos, and Manolis Savvides. The situation worried me since, although I had lost three elite members, my life was in danger if any of them succumbed to the English Holy Inquisition's torture, revealing my hiding place. Fortunately, despite the severe tortures to which they were submitted, nothing was revealed. I was confident that I did not move, even though I was on the alert."*

As revealed by Yiannakis Drousiotis, when he was disheartened by information, some fighters did break down under torture and revealed secrets of the organization; he contemplated, if these elite committed patriots would speak, "for what reason did I come to fight for Cyprus?"

THE RED HOUSE

I presented myself to the Red House. It was located at the

beginning of Nikos Pattichi Street, a few meters after the traffic lights at the junction with Archbishop Makarios Avenue. It was the headquarters of the Special Branch of the "Security Forces," and the director was Douglas Williamson.

Douglas Williamson was well known to my father. He was an active officer of the Anglican Church of Saint Barnabas in Limassol, and in this capacity, he cooperated with the Metropolis of Limassol. At the time, my father was the Hierarchical Commissioner is the responsible for the Limassol District. Williamson was also president of the Limassol Rotary Club from 1955-1956.

He had good knowledge of the Greek language, and the colonial government had appointed him deputy Commander at Platres. (It was there, a month later, 6 November 1956, that he came to a horrible death while trying to open a bomb trap that EOKA had sent to him by post.)

However, this day, he accepted me with, I believe, false courtesy. "Dafni, as you know, in Cyprus these days, theatre is being played. We were surprised to learn that Dafnis Panagides is one of the actors!"

"You are wrong, Mr. Williamson."

"That is what the interrogators in Platres will have to confirm to us!" he said, and he handed me over to the police.

I was kept one night at the Limassol Central Police Station, which was in front of the old Port Customs office. In the same cell was a Mr. Pambos, of the known group of Zacharias criminals from Ypsonas.

"Do you see that person standing on the balcony?" he told me at one point. "Soon, you'll hear his news." A few days later, he was murdered in Limassol, and the crime was attributed to the "Zacharias" gang.

The next day in the morning, I was in a military jeep, escorted by two other jeeps and several armed soldiers en route to Platres.

The International Service of the BBC reported that "in Limassol, a dangerous EOKA terrorist was arrested and his group dismantled." Since then, I have little faith in the BBC news. It was the first time I heard that I was a dangerous terrorist leading a dangerous group.

In the meantime, we had passed Ypsonas village when, for unknown reasons, a message via radio instructed the driver to turn back with the new destination being Omorphita!

THE DETENTION AT OMORPHITA

"Platres" and "Omorphita" were the infamous interrogation centers. They were characterized as EL-DE Haus of Cyprus because of the torture they submitted fighters to extract information for the arrest of Digenis and the suppression of the EOKA struggle. The torture and methods applied by the investigators are described in horrific detail by Frixos Dimitriades in his book Torture: Platres-Omorphita-Lefka. The English journalist Ian Cobain of the prestigious British newspaper The Guardian, in his book Cruel Britannia, A Secret History of Torture, describes this aspect of British history, not only in Cyprus but also in other former British colonies. From inhumane torture in the hands of the interrogators, 14 Cypriot fighters died.

It was physical torture they applied and psychological pressure with the possible risk of unwittingly providing information under the effects of drugs and other things.

Some fighters could not endure the unbearable pain; others attempted to cover their colleagues and deliberately gave information about fighters who had already been arrested or fled abroad. Others gave interrogators misleading testimony. Admiration and respect are born from the resistance to torture by the noble fighters for whom the words of Apostle Paul in his Letter to the Hebrews are applied:

> *"... who through faith conquered kingdoms, enforced justice, received promises, stopped the mouths of lions, quenched raging fire, escaped the edge of the sword, won strength out of weakness, became mighty in war, put foreign armies to flight. Women received their dead by resurrection. Some were tortured, refusing to accept release, that they might rise again to a better life. Others suffered mocking and scourging and even chains and imprisonment. They were stoned, they were sawn in two, they were tempted, they were killed with the sword; they went about in skins of sheep and goats, destitute, afflicted, ill-treated - of whom the world was not worthy - wandering over deserts and mountains, and in dens and caves of the earth."*

With such thoughts and words of prayer, I passed Omorphita Concentration Camp's steps and was led immediately to cell number 2. Soon the door opened, and they brought, to share the cell with me, a known informant of the English, someone we had tried, with Sophocles Potamididae, to kidnap at the organization's request but who had managed to elude us.

Renos Lysiotis, in his book *The Diary of D.P.743*, describes very vividly the experience of our detention in Omorphita and which deserves to be reproduced as he told it. He writes:

> *"It was November 5, 1956, that I was taken downstairs to cell number two, where the heavy door was pulled shut behind me.*
>
> *My cell had two other 'guests.' They introduced themselves; they were both from Limassol. One was called Dafnis; the other answered to the name 'Tsoukas.'*
>
> *'Why were you arrested?' Tsoukas asked me. Dafnis winked at me, and I understood that the young man was a mole.*
>
> *'You're lucky,' Dafnis told me with a grin. 'Our cell is the best. It has only three graves.'*
>
> *I looked around. There stood three cobbled sections in the corners of the cell's concrete floor, which were the right size of graves for people to lay in. There were only two windows, each with two openings covered with iron bars. In the middle of the ceiling was an electric bulb supported with thick wire and nothing else. That was all the furnishing and decoration of the cell. Then I noticed that the walls were full of scratches like someone wanted to skin them a little bit to pierce them, to get out of their grip. I looked closer at the scratches. They were names, dates, and mottos. Everyone who came through here wanted to leave something of his own, signing their names and about their suffering and tortures, hoping to give courage to others who*

would follow. Every scratch on those walls was a reminder of an entire story, a tragic story, a story written in pain and tears.

I glanced at Dafnis, who was watching me with understanding. I took courage and scratched my name over 'my grave.' I also scratched a line recording the date of my imprisonment as, in the cells of Omorphita, it was easy to forget the days."

While I was undergoing long interrogations on the upper floor, on one occasion, Tsoukas approached Reno, another prisoner.

"You know," he says to him, "I am a traitor. They paid me thirty pounds, but I regret my actions. When my parents learned of my deeds, they kicked me out of the house; my fellow-villagers tried to kill me, and those Englishmen deceived me. All I have is a dirty pair of pants and a tornup shirt as property, two or three olives for food, and a grave for home. They promised to send me to England, but first, they want me to tell them more. In your case, try not to say anything. Take an example from me."

I have not seen Tsoukas since. I hear he lives in England. Wherever he is, I hope God is good to him. In our lives, we choose repentance, which is the cornerstone of our Orthodox Christian tradition. It applies to us both.

My interrogations lasted 43 days. They were long and exhausting. Most of the time, they lasted all night. My interrogation was undertaken by George Pereira, whom Renos Lysiotis described as "cunning and intelligent." He spoke Greek very well and presented himself as sympathetic to the Cypriot people's self-determination, "but not with bloodshed, but by peaceful processes."

The material he had at his disposal about me left him no doubt that he had an "EOKA terrorist" in front of him. I was relieved when he understood that the information and the documents he had in his possession had nothing to do with Digenis hiding in our home but focused on the fact that in my house, weapons and ammunition were found that had been imported illegally through the port of Limassol. Other writings found on a bus around Spilia linked me with my brother, Stahis, who was the Leader of the EOKA Youth in Lanition Gymnasium High School and who, in the meantime, had left for studies in the United States. The report found on the bus was referring to the message of Nemesis, the leader of Limassol EOKA, to Digenis, stating, "I entrusted this mission to Adonis, whose brother was remarkable as the head of the youth of his high school, but who, unfortunately, left last week for the U.S. to study." Few students left Cyprus for the USA in those days. This information was enough to decipher my alias: "Adonis."

Describing the life at the Pyla Concentration Camp, Renos Lysiotis writes: "In the dry land locations that were chosen for concentration camps, you found the young and the old, the highly educated and the less educated, enslaved and bonding together, engulfed in their brave Cypriot spirit."

The Detention Camps were indeed a "melting pot" of Cypriots. In Section V of the Pyla Detention Camp, where I was transferred after 43 days of interrogation in Omorphita, I met people from all walks of life. Most of them were there because the British authorities "had valid reasons" to believe that the prisoner was related to the "EOKA terrorist organization." Others were arrested for justifying military operations to "show 'something'," a staged success. All kinds of people were arrested, including known criminals, presented as high-profile members of EOKA. The English believed that announcing the arrests would bend the Spirit of the Cypriots!

The Detention Law entered into force in July 1955. It ruled on the arrest and detention of persons without trial for as long as the British Governor considered it necessary.

The arrival of new prisoners was a big event for the rest of us. "Who are you?" "What news do you bring from the Organization?" "How is the morale of the people?"

In December 1956, four new detainees were brought to our compound. We welcomed them with embraces and tears of emotion. Everyone's morale was so high in and out of the Detention Camp! The experience and emotion brought to mind Vasilis Michaelides' verses from his 1821 poem about the "Race of Romiosini," the race of the Greeks: "Slay us all and let our blood become a river.…Romiosini has been around since the human race began; no one has succeeded in eliminating it because God from up high protects it; Romiosini will perish only when the World ends."

A small bald man with a low creaky voice hugged me and said: "You did not recognize me, Mr. Dafni?"

"No, I do not recall seeing you. Who are you?" I replied.

He was barely able to speak, whispering: "I am Nisiforos from Pachna." He fell unconscious in my arms and collapsed on the ground. He was one of the fighters who had helped build the hideout at the Christodoulides couple's house where Digenis moved his headquarters when he left our house on 14 September 1956. He had suffered such horrible tortures in the hands of the British interrogators at Platres that it had made him unrecognizable! But he did not bend! He did not betray!

Along with Nisiforos, there also arrived the Lambros

brothers, Theodoros Sophocleous and Sofronis Agoystis, all members of Pachna, a place full of action under the EOKA Chief of their area, Lefkios Rodosthenous.

It was true, for those drilled by the English interrogators, what Dante says of those entering Purgatory, "Forget all hope, you who enter here." This also recalled Shiller's saying, "Hope is a falsehood, Death is truth."

Digenis described the 14 fighters who succumbed to the horrific tortures to which they had been subjected. One of them was Vasilis Alexandrou from Limnati, whom I met on a mission entrusted to me in his village.

Digenis writes about Vasilis Alexandrou in his memoirs:

> *"At the start of the struggle, he entered EOKA and developed remarkable exploits as the communication link between the rebel groups of Fassoula and Paramytha. He was arrested and held at the Pyla Detention Facility. Then he was let go but was arrested again and then transferred to the Lanition Gymnasium High School, where he suffered horrific torture. He was transferred to the Polemi Detention Center, where he suffered other severe abuse and beatings. With his health seriously impaired, he was released to his family and died after three days on 21 November 1958."*

The case of Theodosis Hadjitheodosiou from the Village of Stillous is another example of the brutal treatment of EOKA fighters. After being brutally tortured in his home, he was dragged into the street, where he was shot under the guise of attempting escape.

It is admirable that those who bore such torments did not give the investigators information, thereby not damaging the struggle. Others, with weaker characters, broke down and unwittingly gave information, which damaged the fight significantly. I do not blame or judge them. On the contrary, after so many years, I still wake up at night, tormented by the thought that I could not have endured such torture, and what grave consequences would have happened in the struggle to my family and me if, under such torture, I led the English to the headquarters of EOKA in Limassol! Others were "heroes." Still, we "terrorists" fell fighting for the British or were sentenced to death by the Special Courts, which were then set up to suppress the EOKA struggle.

Digenis, as a disciplined and rigorous military man, was relentless and did not accept any mitigating justification for fighters who succumbed under inhuman torture and cracked. One such sad case is that of the fighter, Elias Samaras, an exceptional man who, as a member of his village team in Liopetri, offered, including his entire family, invaluable services to the organization. He was arrested, and under terrible torture, including the administration of chemicals, he revealed the Liopetri barn where four select EOKA fighters were hiding, including his brother, Christos Samaras. They all lost their lives in the epic Battle of the Barn on 2 September 1958.

In a multi-page letter to Pavlos Pavlakis, Elias Samara described in vivid colors and full remorse the conditions under which he succumbed. While the English helped him move to England, he returned to Cyprus and begged Digenis to assign him to a suicide mission so that he could wash away the treachery with his blood. Digenis showed no mercy. Elias was executed under the pomegranate trees in Liopetri. A long time passed before his bones were buried in the cemetery after a church funeral was performed. When alive, he had been the chanter of the Church in his village.

Pavlos Pavlakis described to me the strong feelings he experienced at a memorial service for the Fallen in the Barn of Liopetri when he felt a hand touching him on the shoulder. It was the mother of the two Samaras brothers who asked: *"Tell me, son, I had two sons. One is a hero, the other a traitor. For whom should I light my candle and grieve?"*

THE FIRST VISIT FROM MY WIFE

On her first visit to the Pyla Detention Center, my wife, Maroulla, brought me a note from Digenis. They congratulated me for overcoming the interrogations in Omorphita and appointed me responsible for the Organization at the Pyla Detention Center. About my wife Maroulla, Digenis writes in his memoirs (pp. 225-226):

> "...The guards were Maroulla Daphne Panagides, who kept an eye all day on the British soldiers' movements, keeping us informed of any suspicious moves. Our hostess, Elli Christodoulides, did the same. Both these ladies often saved us from serious dangers. Their readiness to act and their great courage astonished me."

Correspondence with Digenis was transferred in a box full of chocolates which had been modified by my brother-in-law, Andonis Ioannou, the teacher of physics in the Lanition

Gymnasium. The English guards failed to discover that in the innocent box with the chocolates, important documents that could lead to the capture of Digenis had been hidden in its double bottom. In this box, the escape order from Digenis for Andreas Karios, Fotis Pitta, Christakis Tryfonidis, and Frixou Dimitriades was received.

My duties were: 1) informing the Chief about the prisoners' morale, 2) sending reports on the fighters about the interrogations and tortures they suffered (the investigators' questions were indicative of what they knew and where they got the information), and 3) organizing training courses for young detainees who had interrupted their studies and members from the countryside so that the time of detention could be used for their education.

We set up a Committee of the Detained with representatives from each cell compound to communicate with the Detention Center's Management to deal with daily life problems at Pyla. My extremely secret communication with Digenis was only known to Stefanos Protopapas, held in the next cell over from me. A barbed-wire corridor separated us, but we could talk and exchange notes when there was no guard nearby. Stefanos Protopapas succeeded Socrates Loizidis as the General Secretary of (ΠΕΚ) (Cyprus Farmers Organization) following Socrates' arrest the night of 25 January 1955 when the schooner "Saint George" was captured at the coast of Chloraka. Socrates did significant organizational work as the Secretary-General of the (ΠΕΚ) in preparation for the EOKA struggle.

Stefanos chose as his alias "Ω 113". He put as his assistant the late Michalis Eleftheriou. They were both from Polystipos. Michalis Eleftheriou was a person of character, and as a member of the Organization in his community, he had performed multifaceted missions. He worked in the

Detention Center kitchen and had permission to visit all the cells to distribute food. He was an ideal contact link between the prisoners.

GETTING TO KNOW ANDREAS KARIOS

In my same cell was Andreas Karios from Avgorou. From the beginning of our acquaintance, I was impressed by his profound religious faith, patriotism, and dedication to helping improve rural people's living standards. In his village, he was the local PEK Chairman and Secretary of the Religious Orthodox Foundation (ΘΟΙ).

He read chapters from the Bible daily. We were discussing ways to improve the quality of life in the rural world. Which system is best for us in a free Cyprus? The German cooperatives Raiffeisen, the Israeli Kibbutzim, or the Soviet collectives? But no system would be developed, of course, before getting rid of the colonial yoke.

One morning, Andreas told me in confidence that he had written to Digenis asking for permission to escape from the Pyla Detention Center to join rebel groups. Karios could not have imagined that it was through me that his letter had reached Digenis, with my wife, Maroulla, who was the direct link between Digenis and the Detention Facility. Digenis gave his approval for the escape.

The secret escape was via the truck that delivered food to our detention camp, using huge food baskets. This was the idea of Pavlos Pavlakis, Chief of the Kokkinochoria area. Four men were to get into a huge basket in his compound, be covered by bread and watermelons, and be carried by the cooks to the kitchen from where they had access to the truck. The kitchen staff would engage the guards to give the men a chance to enter the truck without being noticed. It was a dangerous undertaking since the sentence, if discovered, was hanging.

Karios was full of joy when he told me that Digenis had chosen him to be one of those who would escape.

A Man's Character:
"Hard to find and understand."

"I want to talk with you in private," Karios told me.

We moved behind the sinks to a place where the armed guards from the surveillance towers could not see us.

"I know," he told me, "that I am undertaking a dangerous mission of life or death.

"I am ready to join the rebels and fight for my homeland's freedom and the glory of Hellenism. I do not know where the Chief will assign me, but we may never see each other again. If this is God's will and you get out of here alive, go to my village, to Avgorou. Meet my wife and kids. Tell them to be proud of their husband and father and that I leave them as a sacred testament, my desire to uphold with honor the name I leave to them. Remind them that 'If we are to die for Greece, the laurel is divine! One only dies once.'"

Karios pulled a paper out of his pocket and put it in my hand.

"I give you," he told me, "this list of my debts, and if it

is God's will to sacrifice my life for the Fatherland, please give this list to my wife and tell her that it is my wish that instead of another memorial service, to pay my debts, to the last penny!"

It is a sad irony comparing the admirable character of Andreas Karios that lifts to the highest ideals of Hellenism, with the scandalous behavior by many in our society today, where we hear people accused of misuse of public and other funds, justifying such action with the excuse that "others stole more"!

The words of Andreas Karios touched my heart as we knelt, praying together, embracing, and kissed each other goodbye. My heart was beating fast, seeing Theodoros Sophocleous and Michali Eleftheriou carrying the basket with Andreas Karios to the kitchen. They passed the first guard and then the second without a problem, as we lost seeing them behind the barbed wire, awaiting in great agony what might happen next. The minutes counted as hours until Michalis Eleftheriou gave us a signal: "Everything went well." The four had entered the food truck without being noticed, leaving the Detention Center with the destination to Liopetri.

The English Guards performed checks every morning and night to find that no prisoner was missing, counting bed heads. We placed watermelon on Kario's bed, saying that he had a strong fever and could not get up to take part in the daily lineup. It took three days to discover that there had been an escape and that four prisoners were missing. The authorities began thorough investigations and imposed punitive measures on all detainees, such as a ban on visits and correspondence for a month.

We were eagerly awaiting the news every night from the controlled government radio. With enthusiasm and applause, we heard the news of the Organization's successes. But on the morning of 2 September 1958, we were shaken when we heard that after a long battle in the barn of Liopetri, four elite fighters of Cypriot freedom had died, including Andreas Karios.

The Battle of the Barn was an example of extraordinary heroism and self-denial, expressing the four fighters' heroic character and personality who shed their blood for Cyprus.

With heavy hearts and tears in our eyes, we gathered on the camp porch where Father Georgios, the young and enthusiastic priest from Sotira (Famagusta), performed the traditional Orthodox memorial funeral service[26].

With Father Georgios, we developed close bonds of friendship because his village was the first village in which my father was appointed teacher after he graduated from the Pancyprian Seminary, which had been founded by the then Bishop of Kition, later the Patriarch of Constantinople, Meletios Metaxakis: The First Among Equals, in the Orthodox Hierarchy[27].

The temperature under the tin roofs made our cells during the summer months unbearable. Sweat flowed endlessly from the face of Father Georgios into his priestly beard while stepping up and down to escape the intolerable heat.

"Father Georgios," I tell him, "Others shed blood; let us not complain about spilling a little sweat. But why don't you sit down and write something about your village and send it to Solomon Panagides to remind him of his years of teaching there?"

---

[26]https://en.wikipedia.org/wiki/Memorial_service_in_the_Eastern_Orthodox_Church
[27]https://en.wikipedia.org/wiki/Eastern_Orthodox_Church_organization

He liked the idea, and to forget the heatwave, wrote a multi-page report about Sotira that I sent to my father, who returned it with a grade of 10 to Father Georgios's joy

The months of detention also impacted the young prisoners who could easily lose their tempers and raise their voices. In one case, Michalakis, known as "Portanzos," criticized Theodoros Sophocleous, who worked in the kitchen, saying that the watermelon he had brought us was not sweet enough. This was enough to provoke a quarrel that woke Theodore up. He was known for his ferocious temperament by the citizens of Pachna, his village. He wasted no time. He threw the watermelon on the ground, stepping on it, exclaiming, "Here, come now to eat sweet watermelon!"

In Kokkinotrimithia

In the Fall of 1958, we were transferred to the Kokkinotrimithia Detention Camp. In the meantime, Sir Hugh Foot was appointed the new Governor, beginning intense behind-the-scenes efforts to find a solution based on Independence.

It was a pleasant day for me when I was visited by Maroulla, who brought our two-year-old daughter, Louisa. As the sun was setting, I heard the loudspeakers calling for Prisoner 722 to go to the Camp Office. My heart was pounding when, with heavy footsteps, I was accompanied by our cell's sergeant to the Camp Office, wondering why I was called. Did they find anything incriminating?

I was led in front of the Camp Commander, who informed me that on her return from her visit to the Detention Center, my wife and child were in a serious car accident near the village of Kofinou, but they were both out of danger. I certainly appreciated this effort to inform me, an act of humanism, but I had great fear and concern that this would not be the whole story. I did not sleep all night. My fellow prisoners stood by me, concerned. The morning after visits began, I received a letter from Maroulla. The small car, driven by Andreas Vassiliou, capsized near a military roadblock in Kofinou. The driver was severely wounded and succumbed to his injuries after a few days at the Limassol Hospital. His name is on the monument honoring the other Freedom Fighters' memory at Kalo Chorio, his village.

Inside the car, besides Maroulla and my young daughter, Louisa, was also Vasiliki, the twelve-year-old daughter of my fellow prisoner and colleague, Sofrone Avgousti, from Pachna.

Maroulla, along with little Louisa, had been ejected several meters into the ditch without serious injuries. But when the Turkish Auxiliary tried to help her get up, she asked anxiously: "The box, the box, where is the box?"

"What is she saying?" the English Sergeant asked the Turkish Auxiliary.

"The poor woman has lost her mind; she is in shock. She does not know what she is talking about. Instead of looking for her baby, she is asking for the chocolate box!"

Maroulla's concern for the box was real. Of course, inside the box was the hidden correspondence from the Detention Camp to General George Grivas-Digenis.

THE AGREEMENTS OF CYPRUS SIGNED. RELEASE OF PRISONERS

In February 1959, the agreements with which the British government granted limited independence to Cyprus and led to the Republic of Cyprus's establishment were signed in Zurich and then in London. As a result of the signing of the agreements, a general amnesty was granted to all detainees. It was an astoundingly historic day! We were received everywhere in an atmosphere of elation, enthusiasm, and celebration.

My father, among his many interests, maintained a large birdcage with many songbirds. After my 33 months of detention, when he welcomed me home, he opened the cage and released all the birds to fly to freedom. Since then, when I hear birds chirping in their cages, I wonder if they are crying for their fate or simply crying to forget their imprisonment. [This story was the inspiration for the book's cover page.]

A DECISIVE MEETING WITH A SHEPHERD

One of my first acts following my release was to go to Avgorou to fulfill the promise I had given to Andreas Karios when he left the camp.

The road to Avgorou was not easy for my small English Ford Prefect with the license plate number 4546. When I realized that I was lost, I saw an old shepherd sitting on a big rock reading a book while his sheep grazed around him. It was a beautiful bucolic scene that many painters would have liked to immortalize. I realized that the book he was holding was the Bible. I waved at him and asked him to tell me the way to the village of Avgoru.

"My blessings, son, but before I show you the way to the village, I want to ask you something. You look like an educated young man from the town. Come and tell me, if our Lord Jesus Christ were the Archbishop of Cyprus, would he be using machine guns and land mines, prosecuting, and killing the English and shedding blood to gain the freedom of Cyprus?"

Immersed in thoughts, I did not venture to answer the shepherd's question.

I arrived in Avgorou, where I met the late fallen patriot's wife, Andreas Karios, and his small children. I shared details about our lives together as prisoners in the Detention Center in a climate of heavy emotion. I communicated his last wishes to pay his debts and honor his legacy.

In the two hours that took me to return to Limassol, the words of the old shepherd were resonating strongly in my mind. Over the years, I asked the same question to many theologians, politicians, and intellectuals. "Is the way to our freedom through violence?" The answers I got did not satisfy me. As a member of the first Cyprus House of Representatives, I objected to creating the National Guard. Instead of a military force, I suggested when I met Makarios, creating task force groups. These teams could contribute to social work in communities or do work in reforestation, elderly care, and the supply of general interest services. I had in mind the Peace Corps that John Kennedy had just created in the United States.

Makarios listened to me carefully. He was a good listener, engaging his interlocutor. He caressed his beard as we drank our coffee. In a moment, he said to me: "Well, my dear Dafni, but what would I do with all those folks who beat on my door every morning asking me to give them a job? The National Guard will absorb a few thousand job seekers." What could I answer to such a Presidential priority?

IS THERE A "RIGHTEOUS WAR"

When in 1997, I first went to Mount Athos[28], I had the good fortune to spend a day with the late elder, Theoklitos, in his cell opposite the Holy Monastery of Saint Dionysius. For company, he had his books and a dozen cats.

Father Theoklitos was a writer of many books and left a significant legacy of texts and studies that enrich the Athonite Orthodox tradition.

I wanted to hear his views on whether we can amend the 6th commandment, from "Thou shall not Kill" instead to "Thou shall not kill unless…" Father Theoklitos' answers to my many questions were clear. Violence is a denial of

[28]https://en.wikipedia.org/wiki/Mount_Athos

the command to love. The Apostle Paul confirms this in his writing to the Romans: "Do not repay anyone evil for evil. Be careful to do what is right in the eyes of everyone. If it is possible, as far as it depends on you, live at peace with everyone. Do not take revenge, my dear friends, but leave room for God's wrath, for it is written: 'It is mine to avenge; I will repay,' says the Lord. On the contrary, if your enemy is hungry, feed him" (Romans 12: 17-20).

The question of whether there is a just war and whether the use of armed violence is justified has occupied philosophers, theologians, and historians through the years.

Is there a "righteous war"? Is taking human life in war a moral act even if you kill for a righteous cause? Does the purpose justify the means?

The Catholic Church accepts "the purpose justifies the means." The Crusades is an example. The Orthodox Church though accepting something similar, under the concept of "«οικονομία» economy," where temporary deviation from orthodox teaching on non-violence may be morally justified but remains a sin.

The church regards abortion as murder, but in the Sunday liturgy, we pray to protect "our land, sea, and air armed forces!".

Elder Sofronios, founder of the Orthodox Monastery of St John the Baptist in Essex, England, does not recite this supplication during the celebration of the Divine Liturgy, considering it contrary to the spirit of love which is the cornerstone of Christian teaching[29].

In Orthodoxy, murder is also a hindrance to sainthood. An

---

[29]https://www.thyateira.org.uk/monastery-of-st-john-the-baptist/

example is Athanasios Diakos, a hero of the Greek war for independence, who has failed since he has taken human lives despite many attempts to be declared a Saint of the Orthodox Church. At the altar of "Righteous Wars", millions of human lives have perished.

The atomic bomb dropped on Hiroshima on August 6, 1945, claimed 210,000 innocent people's lives! An estimated 50-80 million people perished in the Second World War. First, within the Church, to deal with the subject was Holy Saint Augustine (4th century AD), the great Christian writer and apologist. He authored "The State of God," to which Makarios referred in his speech from the Archdiocese balcony on 1 March 1959, promising to make Cyprus a "Nation of God."

"We will make Cyprus a state of progress, a state of prosperity, a Nation of God."

In an interview given by Makarios to the Italian journalist Oriana Falachi, to her question, he replied that the person he most admires in history is Mahatma Gandhi. She did not dare to ask him why because he did not follow the tactic of non-violent Passive Resistance in Cyprus's case.

The pondering that had arisen in me due to the meeting with the old shepherd of Avgorou pushed me to deal systematically with the issues of "War," "Peace," "Violence," "Passive Resistance," "Mahatma Gandhi."

I became a member of the International Organization Against War (War Resister International), which then had its headquarters in London. Unlike the Soviet-inspired World Peace Council, it had no political expediency.

When I hosted the Organization's Secretary in my home, I was informed by a friend who worked in the Cyprus

Intelligence Service that I was blacklisted as left-leaning and likely a "Crypto Communist"! The truth is that I took part in and addressed greetings to the Great Peace Demonstration organized by the World Peace Council (WPC) in Limassol in 1964 against the British bases. The WPC was driven by the Soviet Union. Its Secretary of the Cyprus branch was my House of Representatives col league, Giangos Potamitis. Mikis Theodorakis was among the speakers at the Limassol demonstration.[30]

As I write in the following pages, the armed struggle was a mistaken political choice, even more so with the Church leading the way, as evidenced by the result. This, of course, in no way diminishes our admiration for the EOKA fighters in their heroism, self-denial, and love for the Motherland.

I consider the use of all forms of violence as a breach of moral law.

---

[30]https://en.wikipedia.org/wiki/World_Peace_Council

CHAPTER THREE - 1959-1960

AN IMPORTANT INTERVAL.

If a good day can be seen in the morning, the gloomy future of the newly created Republic of Cyprus was evident even before dawn.

The months following the signing of the Zurich-London Agreements in February 1959 until the official proclamation of the Republic of Cyprus on 16 August 1960 were, in my view, crucial for the future course of the Republic. If we consider that the Agreements were the architectural designs, the interval that followed was when the foundations were laid out and which turned out to be fragile

From very early, it was evident that neither the Greek Cypriots nor the Turkish Cypriots accepted the agreements as the final solution to the Cyprus problem. It was merely a temporary respite for both sides that would lead to new struggles for the final "victory," which, for the Greek Cypriots, was the Union with Greece, and for the Turkish Cypriots Partition.

The historian Petros Savvidis did an in-depth analysis of

the events that preceded the collapse of the Agreements on the eve of Christmas 1963.

Speaking at the University of Nicosia on 28 November 2014, drawing mainly from Turkish sources and documents that were largely unknown to Greek Cypriots, he wrote that as far back as one year before the signing of the Zurich-London Agreements, Turkish Major Ismail Tansu-Dogan had already drawn up a plan to repossess Cyprus for Turkey.

As Major Tansu revealed in his memoirs, at the end of 1959, there were 5,000 trained Turkish Cypriot fighters in Cyprus with the aim, by the end of 1960, to increase this number to 10,000. With the raising of the Cyprus flag at the Governorate on August 16, 1960, there were in Cyprus, in the hands of Turkish Cypriot, 2,997 English rifles, 6,800 grenades, 877 pistols, 747 automatics rifles, 96 Bren guns, and 1,348,000 cartridges.

At this same time, the situation on the Greek Cypriot side was different. While EOKA had disbanded and surrendered almost all of its weaponry, new armed groups were appearing, which could be described as personal "chiefdoms" - the main of these parastate groups led by Nikos Samson, Vassos Lyssaridis, and the Interior Minister, Polykarpos Giorkatzis. The parastate organization of Polykarpos Giorkatzis was considered the most important. His group was known as AKRITAS, which was the nickname of its Chief. "AKRITAS" Chief of Staff was 'Nikos Kosis, later a Minister of the Interior. In an interview with Petros Savvidis, Nikos Kosis said the Organization had about 10,000 registered members and about 670 weapons.

In other words, while Greeks and Turks agreed to work jointly to build Cyprus as a democratic state, we were preparing its collapse, ready to exterminate each other.

Here we must stress that while the sole aim of Partition united Turkish Cypriots with full dependence on Turkey, the Greek Cypriots were divided into factions with a view to fratricidal division and personal dominance. They used "self-defense" from the Turks as a pretext, resulting in hundreds of well-meaning young people believing that they were serving national interests when, in fact, they were instruments for promoting ideological goals and personal ambitions, validating the words of the Bible: *"every kingdom divided is driven to destruction, and every city of the house divided will not stand"* (Matthew 12:15).

ESTABLISHMENTS OF CLANDESTINE POLITICAL MOVEMENTS AND PARAMILITARY GROUPS

With the common understanding of Makarios and Grivas, the EDMA political party was founded on 1 April 1959 to absorb the members of EOKA and support Makarios in building the Republic of Cyprus. It was a summer's daydream. In less than three months from Independence, Hellenism's historical nemesis, called "Division," was taking root between those who disagreed with the compromises Makarios agreed to in signing the Zurich- London Agreements, declaring that they would continue the unyielding fight for Union with Greece. A concerted effort by the pro-Makarios forces, along with censorship and suppression of free dialogue, deepened the rift between Makarios and Grivas in Cypriot Hellenism.

General Grivas' misguided decision to enter Greek politics contributed further to this division. He was seduced by the politicians of Greece with the idea of "Saving Greece." He was eventually forced to withdraw his name, and with it, his reputation was tarnished. It was then that the experienced politician, George Papandreou, coined the characterization of

Grivas in the saying, *"Grivas was admired when in hiding."*

A review of the period preceding the proclamation of the Republic of Cyprus shows that:

As already mentioned, neither the Greeks nor the Turks of Cyprus intended to implement the Constitution agreed upon with the Zurich agreements. Both ethnic communities accepted the agreements as a temporary stopover toward their final goal: Union with Greece for the Greeks and Partition for the Turks.

The Greek Cypriot side was torn apart and divided. Instead of the goal being for Cyprus's good, the goal turned out to be how to dominate and destroy each other.

On their part, the Turkish Cypriots were waiting for an opportunity for an armed conflict and were preparing for it. A confidential document was found with the Turkish Cypriot Minister of Agriculture, Fazil Plumer, dated 14 September 1963 and signed by Fazil Kuchiuk, the Republic of Cyprus's vice-president, and the President of the Turkish Community Assembly, Rauf Denktash. It mentioned, among other things, the following:

> *"The Zurich-London Agreements were accepted as a 'temporary transitional post,' and for this reason, we signed them. We would prolong the quarrels between the two communities for a while, raising the issue of Partition at the United Nations, asserting that 'the Agreements are unworkable.' The reason that we signed the Agreements is that: a) the agreements recognized the rights of Turkey internationally over Cyprus, and b) we will take advantage of the mistakes and blunders*

*of the Romious [Romans],[31] and when we
are better prepared, we will wait for the day
when they want to modify the Agreements, to
achieve our full freedom."*

The full document is set out in Annex VIII of Christodoulou
Benjamin's book "The Difficult Years". "Τα Δύσκολα
Χρόνια."

Should we consider this document a prophetic revelation
or admit that the Turks knew us better than we knew ourselves?

Importantly, Turkey, which had drawn up a plan for
occupation and partition of Cyprus since 1955, remained
adamant in this aim in contrast to the Greek Cypriot side,
which time and again muddled its political objectives...a
behavior that continues until today. Regardless of which of
the goals was the "desired" or the "feasible," our dealing with
the national issue has been inconsistent and amateurish. The
wise, experienced Mayor of Nicosia, Themistocles Dervis,
captured this predicament in his characterization of Makarios'
first Cabinet, referring to it as a "Children's Choir."

THE PROCLAMATION OF THE REPUBLIC OF CYPRUS

As 16 August 1960 approached, my concern for the future
of Cyprus grew. Were the struggles and slogans a dream,
a hollow delusion, or would we be entering a period of
happiness, peace, and prosperity? Would we be able to build
on the sacrifices of the many? "A prosperous righteousness,

---

[31] https://translate.google.com/
translate?hl=en&sl=el&u=https://www.oodegr.com/oode/
istoria/rwmi/ti_einai_rwmiosyni_1.htm&prev=search

a State of God" as Makarios promised?

After 33 months of detention, it was time for me to focus on my family and my work. My imprisonment in the Cells of Omorphita, Pyla, and Kokkinotrimithia deprived me of my two daughters and my wife and negatively affected the small business I had started, importing and selling tiller tractors for agriculture. I was determined to rebuild my business and look after my family. Perhaps because I did not consider the Republic of Cyprus's proclamation as an occasion for celebrations, I left for Germany, looking after my business. A few days after the proclamation, I was in London, where I met with Giannis Stais.

I knew Giannis Stais, who had a citrus farm near to ours. He had bought a tractor from me for his estate and appreciated my help to his Farm Manager while he was in London, where he owned one of the more aristocratic restaurants, The White Tower.

He invited me to lunch at his restaurant on Percy Street. I was impressed by the luxury. I was not accustomed to this way of life. I grew up in simplicity, and the beauty of nature and life in big cities made me uncomfortable.

"What do you say we start with an appetizer salad of avocado and shrimp?" He asked gently. I froze a bit because I had never tried this exotic appetizer in my life.

"If you suggest it, okay!" I said, and so I tried shrimp-avocado salad for the first time in my life!

Mr. Stais knew of my participation in the liberation struggle of 1955-59, and we quickly entered the topic. "In the very chair where you are sitting now, last Thursday, was Mr. Hugh Foot, with the Labor Party executives," Mr. Stais said. Hugh Foot was the last English Governor of Cyprus. He had taken part in the Zurich talks in London and worked closely with Makarios.

At some point, Mr. Stais continued. "Mr. Foot asked me how I felt about the Cyprus Agreement." "What do I know" I replied. "Once our Leader Makarios has signed it, we have full confidence in him."

Then Mr. Foot went on, "You know, Mr. Stais, I asked Makarios this same question following the signing of the Agreements, as we were leaving Lancaster House. 'Your Holiness,' I told him. 'How do you feel now that you signed the Agreements?'"

"I was disturbed by the answer that The Archbishop gave me. 'It is not what we expected. But the Turks are known for their feeble intelligence. In time we will take back what we are entitled to and what they have taken from us with this agreement,' was Makarios' reply."

"His response disturbed me," Foot said, "as it showed that his intentions were not honest. I asked you this same question, wanting to see if other Cypriots had the same feelings."

Mr. Stais was a reputable and trustworthy gentleman, devoted to his work, a man without political ambitions. I had no reason to doubt the authenticity of his conversation with Hugh Foot. I tried to cross-check this information, but I could not find anything to confirm that Makarios signed the Agreements under pressure with the ulterior motive to overthrow them when he had the opportunity.

However, in his public speeches and statements, as well as his sermons such as that in Yialousa, he clearly stated that the goal of the struggle remained the Union with Greece as well as his decision to oppose the implementation of the Zurich Agreement provision for separate Municipalities for the Turkish Cypriots. Such statements do not leave any doubt that Makarios believed he had the power to "get back" a lot of what the Greek Cypriots conceded to Turkey with Zurich.

Mr. Stais' conversation put me in deep thoughts. I do not hide the fact that we all had been disappointed with the result of the struggle, but he thought that Makarios would find a way to get us out of the humiliation we felt with the Zurich Agreements, gave me some relief.

Many torturing questions were turning in my mind for weeks and months. Does Makarios have new designs? Will he soon invite us to new struggles? What role will Digenis have?

When I returned to Cyprus from London, the Republic of Cyprus was already a historical reality. Makarios was the President, Dr. Koutsuk was the vice president. There was a mixed Ministerial Council of Greek and Turkish Ministers, a House of Representatives and a Greek Cypriot, and a Turkish Cypriot Community Assembly.

That September, I was in the Kakomalis Forest when I noticed from a distance that Chrysoula Petropoulou and Elizabeth Nicolaou were approaching. They were both devoted members of the Christian movement. Chrysoula from Greece was a teacher of secondary education at the Gymnasium of Limassol. She was a woman of strong patriotic and Christian feelings and a good friend. Elizabeth, shy and kind, offered valuable services as a liaison with the Digenis Headquarters in Limassol, working closely with Maroulla.

"What are you doing up here, Mr. Daphne? Cyprus needs you. We need you to run for a seat in the House of Representatives."

"God forbid, Miss Chrysoula, never! My irrevocable

decision is to work for my family and my business."

She explained that with Limassol MP, Andreas Papadopoulos, as Minister of Communications and Works, a seat in the House of Representatives was vacated. It was the general wish of the patriotic forces for me to take it.

She couldn't convince me. In the days that followed, I received strong pressure to accept. My good friend, Theodoros Papas, who was a member of the Greek Community Assembly, played an important role in convincing me to run, reminding me that "We began a journey for the struggle for freedom, and now that Cyprus needs us, we cannot abandon her."

Metropolitan Anthimos of Kitium invited me to his office, also urging me to accept. "We have received appeals from all over and from the countryside. Everyone wants you in the House."

"But your Holiness, I have no knowledge about politics, nor do I know how to make public speeches," I replied.

He smiled and, with humor, conveyed his recipe on how to become great in politics.

"Go," he told me, "to Andrea Ioannidis' bookstore and get a copy of the Cyprus Constitution. Read it two or three times, and you will be an expert. As for speeches, when you present yourself in front of a crowd, and, since your profession is gardening, instead of seeing the heads of people, imagine that you have in front of you heads of cabbage." I laughed from my heart, and when saying goodbye, I told him, "It is OK; tell His Beatitude that I consent."

A few days later, I got a phone call from Mr. Stelios Michaelides, a House of Representatives member, asking to meet him that afternoon at the Yacht Club. The meeting was with the other members of the House of Representatives of the Limassol Patriotic Front Andonis Anastasiadis, Emilios Frangos, and Christodoulos Michaelides.

"Listen," he said. "A serious problem has been created that endangers the unity of our party. Azinas does not accept Daphnes Panagides, and he is urging Makarios to support the nomination of Panayiotis Orfanos."

Azinas had played an important role in the purchase, marketing, and importation of weapons during the EOKA Struggle and had close ties to both Grivas and Makarios. It was understandable to have demands to satisfy his policies and ambitions. Many of the EOKA senior leaders, with the coming of independence, were seeking positions of power in the new order, placing supporters in key positions, and in several cases, organizing their partisan organizations and armed gangs.

The Limassol MPs were in a difficult position. Doctor Emilios Frangos, in his intervention at the meeting, commented that any retreat on our part to meet Azina's request was unacceptable. "Today," he said, "I had a delegation from Pyrgos in my office, telling me they would not accept the dictates of ΠΕΚ (to support Orfanos), as they were supporting Dafnis Panagides' candidacy." Christodoulos Michaelides, the founder of ΣΕΚ, was even more emphatic. "We do not accept Azina's interference in our district, period. Our members insist on Daphne's candidacy."

"Let's call Glafkos to convey to him the position of our District," said Stelios Michaelides, and so he got Glafkos, the House President, on the phone. Glafkos was in constant contact with Makarios, who totally controlled the public, up to who would be hired, from the highest position down to the House's cleaners and cafeteria personnel.

Stelios Michaelides seemed disturbed by his phone

conversation with Glafkos. "Makarios does not want to rebuff Azina's wishes, he told us when he had finished. Glafkos advises us to persuade Dafnis to withdraw, and if we fail, to avoid, as the Limassol MP's, taking a position for either candidate."

The Limassol MPs unanimously disagreed with Glafkos' recommendation. "We," said Christodoulos Michaelides, "receive pressures daily from the Trade Unions and the Pancyprian Farmers' Union of Cyprus. They insist on the candidacy of Dafnis." The other Limassol MPs agreed, and so we went to the elections with me as the candidate.

I left the meeting feeling a sense of relief. I was entering the elections not as a candidate of the National Democratic Front for Reconstruction (EDMA), a patchwork of organizations that supported Makarios and the Government, but with wide support from the town and the countryside. I had every right to present myself and to be independent.

"You can tell a good day from how it looks in the morning," my

beloved grandfather Socrates reminded me. Was I entering a world with behaviors incompatible with my principles and character? Unfortunately, my fears of the 'process' were indeed being confirmed, as you will see.

CHAPTER FOUR

THE CYPRUS HOUSE OF REPRESENTATIVES

ELECTED MEMBER OF THE
FIRST CYPRIOT HOUSE OF REPRESENTATIVES

On sunday, 25 september 1960, I won the alternate election in the Limassol District. The following Wednesday, I took the oath to become a member of the first Cyprus House of Representatives.

Below I will share some of my experiences as a member of the First House of Representatives, which was the only one operating under the Zurich Constitution's provisions, with 35 Greek Cypriots and 15 Turkish Cypriot MPs.

I joined the House with the best of intentions. I believed that I could improve the rural population and the working class that lived under difficult circumstances. Together with members of SEK and PEK from Famagusta and Limassol, such as Kostas Christodoulides, Andreas Vassiliou, Nikos Angelidis, Kyriakos Economou, Abraham Vassiliou, Eugenios Kotsapas, Takis Mereditetis, Evgenios Petros from the Prastio Avdimou, Theophanis Abraham from Pachna,

Panteleakis Diamantis, we put forward the "Agro-Workers Cooperation" law. We aimed to support the training of leaders in the principles of Democracy and Democratic Socialism. Not long after, we learned that both the Authorities of the British Bases and our Ministry of Interior with Minister Polycarpos Georagatzis had instructed their agents to report on the issues and discussions we had every Tuesday Limassol Office of the Cyprus Workers Federation. Our request to establish a cooperative farm in Akrotiri to restore 20 families of fighters fell into the void when the Bishop of Kitium, Anthimos, called me to his office, telling me to drop it, as he considered it to be communist-like, and that he would proceed as a Metropolis to create the farm. And our request for the establishment of a Cooperative Society for Rural Development was not approved by the Commissioner for Cooperation, Andreas Azinas.

But our plans for rural development did become known. One morning there came to my office a representative from Caterpillar, the American tractor company.

"I have some good news for you. Our Company is ready to undertake the education of your two daughters in America when they are ready to enter a university."

Christmas was approaching when a taxi stopped outside my house, and the driver told me he had a box for me. It was a Telefunken radio music set, a "Christmas Gift" by a German who represented Cyprus's German interests. Both Caterpillar and Telefunken's offers were rejected!

The President of the Chambers of Commerce and Industry was then my colleague in the House, Michalakis Savvidis. He was also the Chairman of the Bank of Cyprus, in which I kept a current account with a significant debit balance. He asked to see me in private.

At our meeting, he asked for my vote in the House of Representatives for a bill he had proposed (tabled) that included anti-labor provisions. I promised that he would have my vote, but I pretended that, for health reasons, I had to be in Athens…so as not to be in the House when that bill came up for a vote.

In another case, one of my employees informed me that he had to assassinate someone in Limassol. "Who gave you such instructions?" I asked him.

"The Chief," he answered me.

"But what Chief, Michalakis?," I asked him. "Digenis is in Athens. I will report you to the police if you commit the crime."

He smiled. "When you know who gave the orders, you will close your mouth."

Better not to know, I thought. A few days later, while I was driving from Nicosia, I heard in the radio that the crime was committed in Limassol.

LIAR WANTED

A few weeks had passed since my election to the House of Representatives when my friend, agronomist Kostas Afamis, called me one day.

"Do not miss," he told me, "the hilarious comedy 'Seeking a Liar,' that is being played these days at the Yiordamply Theater. You are a beginner in politics, and you need to take lessons for your House of Representatives duties."

In the plot, the actor who declares as his main occupation, "Liar," is the Director of an MP's office in Athens to justify the blatantly unrealized promises of the MP to his voters.

I went to see this movie with my friend and fellow MP Antonaki Anastasiadis. Apart from our laughs, we were concerned that what the film presented was a true depiction of Greece's political reality. I could not imagine that such behaviors were taking place in our Presidential Palace. And I do not hide the fact that I, too, often have had to justify unfulfilled promises to my constituents, pretending various excuses.

An example shared by Haris Gavrielides, godfather to my brother's son, Alexis, indicates political falsification and lying by the wicked. Haris was the first Director of the Cyprus Central Bank. Early one morning, his phone rang with Makarios calling, inquiring why "a brilliant" applicant from Panayia (Makarios' village) was not hired as a secretary by the Bank.

"Your Holiness, her written exam was one of the worst," Haris replied, upset for such petty meddling in his work.

A few minutes later, the phone rang again. "Haris, forget my earlier call; her father was here with me."

No doubt, the unassuming villager returned to Panayia pleased by the reception and response he found from the President himself.

Unfortunately, such incidents are not isolated. To a certain extent, none of us in the House were innocent of giving promises that have never been fulfilled.

The rural population was struggling. Agricultural debts, viticulture, irrigation, and infrastructure were only a few of the many problems we were dealing with in the first House of Representatives.

One Sunday, I joined Makarios in Kalo Chorio, Limassol, which is my village of origin.

After the Divine Liturgy, we sat at the café for coffee. "Your Holiness, when is electricity coming, when can we expect water in the homes, when is the Regional Health Center coming, we need the paving of the road to Limassol, when will you build the Regional School, when will you receive our Commandaria [32]and a lot more?!"

Makarios, with his magnetic smile and humor, answered:

"What can I do? The Government is to be blamed!"

Vasilis Kastanis, sitting next to me, whispered in my ear. "But Daphne, can you tell me who is … this government?" Makarios overheard this as he looked at us and smiled!

WORKING AT THE HOUSE OF REPRESENTATIVES

Meanwhile, the work of the House proceeded, and the first year passed without special events. We were all inexperienced. Besides the AKEL team with specific goals and political aspirations, the rest went to the House because we believed that we had done important work for Cyprus or personal ambitions or the psychological need for projection. This latter was why almost all of us were competing on who would ask the ministers most questions. We felt the greatest satisfaction when, on the following day, we often saw in big letters our name in the newspapers or heard it on the radio. "The Honorable Member of the Limassol Region asks the Honorable Minister of Agriculture, 'Minister, when will you finally build some dams to solve the water problem?'"

[32]https://en.wikipedia.org/wiki/Commandaria

When will you…? finally solve the Viticulture (problem), electrification? Access? Build the hospital in Asgata…?

In village cafes, the questions were immensely popular, and the number of items depended heavily on how popular a member was.

I visited the first Minister of Finance one day, Mr. Riginos Theocharous.

He told me the Beatitude instructed him to submit a rough estimate of the works demanded by the MPs for the current year.

"Well, tell your other colleagues we need 60 budgets to do what they want."

HOUSE OF REPRESENTIVES VISIT TO ISRAEL

At breakfast in March 1962, I received a call from Glafkos Clerides, the House President.

"When you come to the House," he told me, "pass by my office. I want to discuss something personal with you."

I met Glafkos Clerides the next day, who told me that His Beatitude wishes to accept Israel's invitation for an official House of Representatives delegation visit to the neighboring country. But there were strong reactions from AKEL and from his personal physician, Dr. Vasos Lyssarides. Besides, MPs did not want to associate their name with Israel to offend the Arabs with whom Cyprus had excellent relations.

I said without hesitation that I was willing to join a House of Representatives delegation to visit Israel. We had a lot to learn from Israel's technology in managing water resources and its agricultural and cooperative infrastructure.

The next day, the newspaper Last Hour called me a paid NATO agent! When, after a few years - in 1974, I was recruited as the Director of the "Fasouri Fruit Company," one of my first steps was to remove its name from the blacklist in the Arab world. The Farm, known as Fasouri, was founded by Jews and was named "Cypriot- Palestinian Plantations." When I visited Damascus, at the Agency's offices responsible for the matter, I was not surprised to learn that a small percentage of the Fasouri exports (if I remember 2-3%) had to be paid to some organizations in Cyprus. The "Last Hour" newspaper was among the recipients!

We were cordially welcomed in Israel and were impressed both by the hospitality and the Israelis' achievements. Among them were the cooperative farms known as Kibbutz. The high point of our visit, on my part, was our visit to Ben Gurion, Founder of the State of Israel and its first Prime Minister.

He lived in a simple little house in a kibbutz and accepted us in his simple office. I was impressed by his many white hairs and his piercing gaze. But I felt "shock" when he welcomed us by speaking in ancient Greek instead of another language. I was ashamed. I graduated from the Greek Gymnasium of Limassol, and without wanting to boast, I was a good student, but I did not understand what Ben Gurion was telling us. Next to me was Nikos Angelidis.

"Nick," I asked him, "what is he saying?"

"I'll tell you later," he replied. Ben Gurion was citing a text from the Neoplatonic Alexandrian philosopher Plotinus.[33]

When I returned to Cyprus, I did not waste time. I went to see my friend's Andreas Ioannidis bookstore and asked his recommendations for books of ancient writers circulating at

---

[33] https://en.wikipedia.org/wiki/Plotinus

the time.

"Ancyra" had just published a complete set of ancient writers with text, comments, and translations. I bought the series without hesitation. It cost 75 pounds. (My House of Representative's allowance was then 97 pounds.) This series still graces my library

INTERNATIONAL LABOR CAMP AT DALI

The National Youth Council was the coordinating body of many Organizations and Associations. Its Secretary was Mikis Michaelides, who at the time worked at the Foreign Ministry. I was responsible for International Relations. After the violent intercommunal conflict on Christmas Eve 1963 and the tension created by the Turkish Cypriot MPs' withdrawal from the House of Representatives and the Government, we decided to organize an International Camp of Volunteers to promote inter-communal cooperation[34]. As the camp project, we chose to clean the road that connected Dali, a Greek Cypriot village, with Louroujina, a purely Turkish Cypriot village. Previously, I took part in Volunteer Camps in Europe and maintained close ties with both the World Council of Churches and UNESCO. Volunteer Camps were an important activity of these two Organizations.

We named the road "Friendship Road." It was widely publicized both in Cyprus and abroad for this initiative. In August 1964, the camp was housed in the school building offered by the village of Idaliou with about 25 volunteers from many countries. We did not have Turkish Cypriot participants, but one afternoon a Turkish Cypriot youngster came to meet me. "My name is Dervis Kavasoglou. I am a

[34]https://en.wikipedia.org/wiki/Bloody_Christmas_(1963)

member of the Turkish Cypriot Trade Union belonging to the PEO, and I came to see what you are doing." I was impressed by the wholesomeness of Dervis Kavazoglou. That meeting was the beginning of a close friendship and cooperation between us until his brutal murder by the Turkish extremist organization, T.M.T[35], on 11 April 1965, together with his fellow trade unionist, Kostas Miaiaoulis. My friendship with Kavazoglou became even closer when we were both members of the Cyprus delegation to the Global Forum of Young Communists in Moscow in September 1964.

AN ENGLISHMAN WANTS TO JOIN THE CAMP

A few days before the start of the Camp, I was having a coffee in a patisserie on Ledra Street near the Pancyprian Youth Council's offices when a small, totally unknown fellow came into the patisserie and up to me. "Do you speak English?" he asked me.

"A little," I said. "How can I help you?"

He gave me a note on which the name "Dafnis Panagides" was written.

"Do you know where I can find this person? They told me that I could find him in the House, but the House telephone operator had not seen him in the morning and said he had left for the National Youth Council, whose offices are somewhere here nearby."

"Yes," I'll tell him. "I am familiar with his name, although I have not met him personally. But why do you want to see

[35] https://en.wikipedia.org/wiki/Turkish_Resistance_Organisation

him?"

He showed me a fragment from the London Times that referred to the Dali International Work Camp and its purpose to help create a climate of cooperation and peaceful coexistence between the two Cyprus communities.

"My family roots are from the Island of Chios," he said. "My grandfather survived the 1822 massacres of the Greek population by the Ottoman Turks[36], and I have donated my property to a Christian organization engaged in reconciliation and peace in areas where there is racial hatred, prejudice, and war. The organization is named 'Christian International Peace Service (CHIPS)' and has as its mission the words of Jesus: 'Blessed are the peacemakers, for they will be called sons of God' (Matthew 5:9). I came to Cyprus to participate in the Friendship Camp that you are organizing."[37]

I was impressed by Roy Calvocoressi - that was his name, but I still remembered my experiences of the EOKA struggle, and I thought he could be a man from British Espionage. Moreover, let us not forget that the Devil, to achieve his diabolic purposes, often appears as an "Angel of Light"!

I tried to hold back my feelings and proceeded:

"Listen, my friend." I'll tell him, "In fact, I'll leave for Limassol shortly, so if you want to come with me, I'll introduce you to him."

He accepted my proposal, and soon we took the road to Limassol. As he confessed to me later, he was afraid that I would kidnap him at some point.

We went straight to my house, where I introduced him to the father of Dafnis Panagides, who just happened to be the

[36]https://en.wikipedia.org/wiki/Chios_massacre
[37] https://chipspeace.org/who-we-are/

driver who brought him from Nicosia! What followed was difficult to describe. Roy explained it as Divine intervention.

We became dear friends and worked internationally in areas where there was racial or other discrimination, in the Philippines, Africa, the United Kingdom, and Cyprus.

He was the son of a wealthy family in London with an important financial background that he donated to the promotion of peace based on the Christian principle that, "There is neither Jew nor Gentile, neither slave nor free, nor is there male and female, for you are all one in Christ Jesus" (Letter to the Galatians 3:28).

A team of volunteer members of the organization led by him settled in the village of Kidasi in Paphos and another group in Lefka to preserve orchards abandoned by their Greek and Turkish owners for safety reasons. Volunteers watered the trees and looked after them, hoping that the intercommunal conflicts were transient and that the legitimate owners would return to their property in safety. Unfortunately, this did not work out.

This action was highly appreciated by both Greek Cypriots and Turkish Cypriot owners. But neither Rauf Denktash nor Polycarpos Georatzis favorably viewed Roy's organization as genuine with sincere intentions promoting inter-community friendship. The Interior Ministry expelled Roy Calvocoressi from Cyprus on the suspicion that he was a spy of the Turks!

The eulogy of Dafnis at Roy's funeral in London reveals these two peacemakers' deep friendship fostering understanding and cooperation in discrimination and conflict areas based on the Christian principle of love.[38]

[38]See Annex 3: The deep relationship between Roy Calvocoressi and Dafnis Panagides revealed in DP's tribute at Roy's funeral in London, England on 4th October 2012

AT THE YOUTH FORUM IN MOSCOW (SEPTEMBER 1964)

One of my colleagues in the House was Chrysis Dimitriades, a wellknown lawyer from Limassol who was Secretary of EDON, the large Youth Organization affiliated with AKEL. Chrysis invited me to represent the National Youth Council at the International Communist Youth Forum on September 16-23 in Moscow. The Cypriot delegation participants, besides the EDON team, included the theologian and close associate of Archbishop Makarios, Urania Kokkinou, and Dervis Kavazoglou.[39]

A few days before our departure for Moscow, the Soviet Ambassador invited me to his office. He wanted my visit to the Soviet Union to be an opportunity to see the achievements of Communism.

He was very polite and listened to me with interest.

"I would thank you Mr. Ambassador if you would allow me to personally see four things during my visit: 1). An agricultural collective; 2.) A school; 3.) A church; 4.) A visit to a Soviet family."

"You will have the chance to do everything," he told me and wished me a good trip.

DERVIS KAVAZOGLOU

Kavazoglou and I shared the same room in the hotel "Ukraine," where we had the opportunity to discuss many issues, even things of our personal life. I was impressed by his character's integrity and his intense concerns regarding

[39]https://en.wikipedia.org/wiki/Dervi%C5%9F_Ali_ Kavazo%C4%9Flu

Cyprus's social and political problems. He was sensitive to the workers' issues, and, as a member of the Turkish Trade Unions, he had a rich experience with the labor struggles. He was particularly sensitive to principles and morals. When, one night, he realized that members of the delegation were hanging out with young girls of the Komsomol,[40] he felt deeply disappointed and pessimistic about the future of Cyprus. With some prophetic intuition, he said to me: "Daphne, God will one day destroy us."

At the Forum, our relationship with Kavazoglou impressed the thousands of representatives from all the World countries. Our photo was published on the front page of "Pravda," sending the message of friendship and cooperation between Greeks and Turks in Cyprus.

VISITING MAKARIOS WITH KAVAZOGLOU

When we returned to Cyprus, the planting season was approaching. In early November, Kavazoglou came to see me in Limassol.

"I must see Makarios. It is a matter of urgency. The farmers of Lurutzina and other Turkish Cypriot villages are desperate because the Cooperative Bank is not giving them the fertilizers and seeds for this planting season. They claim that they have instructions from Makarios to not provide fertilizers and seeds to Turkish Cypriots this year. The followers of Denktash, who was opposed to Greek-Turkish cooperation, were exploiting this situation."

I telephoned the Presidential Palace straight away.

---

40 https://en.wikipedia.org/wiki/Komsomol

Makarios gave us an appointment the next morning. With us would be the Mayor from Lurutzina and the Secretary of the Turkish Co-operative. We would also be accompanied by Professor Fivos Kotsapas of the Pedagogical Academy, a staunch supporter of Greek-Turkish cooperation.

In the morning, we went to Makarios's office. He was very cordial to us. We all kissed his hand in the Cyprus tradition of respect. Kavazoglou brought up the issue. The Turkish farmers were in despair. The rains had come. They had no seeds or fertilizers, and they would lose the growing season. It would be a financial disaster for them and a triumph for Denktash and his like-minded men.

Makarios listened carefully. At some point, he hit his desk with his hand such that the cup of coffee was overturned. He raised his voice and said in intense style:

"These are Azina's machinations. I did not know about this, but I will order them to give you immediately whatever seeds and fertilizer you need."

We felt very satisfied. Kavazoglou called me the next day to tell me that everyone in the Lurutzina cafe was speaking favorably, with flattering words about Makarios.

The Turkish Cypriot mayor from Lurutzina prepared the Turkish Cypriots list to receive grain seeds and fertilizers for the new year's cultivation.

Unfortunately, the Turkish Cypriots of Lurutzina are still waiting for seeds and fertilizers that never came. The followers of TMT and Denktash were delighted. For them, this was an example of the future that awaited the Turkish Cypriots under a government by Makarios and his Greek Cypriot-controlled government.

I felt deep frustration, but I did not know what to say to

Kavasoglou. I covered up for Makarios with a fake story. I said fertilizers and seeds were loaded, but the Greek Cypriot drivers refused to transfer them to Lurutzina because they were afraid of an attack by Denktash supporters. I tried to cover up the scam — and felt the burden of my guilt.

ELECTRIFICATION OF A TURKISH CYPRIOT VILLAGE

It was not long after the fertilizers that were never delivered that I visited the Technical Director of the Cyprus Electricity Authority in Famagusta, the engineer Petros Petrides, a relative and friend who shared the following incident. His boss, the Famagusta Electricity Authority director, called him one day and ordered him to install electric power in a Turkish Cypriot village that same day. When the engineers observed that this could not be done in one day as it takes time to draw up the plans, receive permits, and do a safe installation of the poles, the Director informed emphatically: "Listen, Petro, we have been ordered by the Archbishop, who is in New York and wants us to take electricity to the Boggasi village today because the Turks complained to the UN that we do not provide them with electricity." A United Nations mission will visit the area shortly to assess what is happening. We want them to see that Turkish Cypriots are treated well by the government.

The Director set aside the normal process, responding to the President's order. Archbishop Makarios followed up with Petro urging him to "Install 2-3 poles and a few wires, just enough for the UN visitors to see and take pictures."

With such behavior by those at the top of the newly born Republic of Cyprus, it is no wonder that the Turkish Cypriots turned to Turkey for a better chance to get their electricity than from their own government, as it happened with their water supply, that comes to occupied Cyprus these days from Southern Turkey, through a pipeline under the Mediterranean Sea.[41]

PAVING THE ROAD TOWARDS KELLAKI VILLAGE

A delegation from Kellaki village headed by the bus driver running the daily route to Limassol came to my office. They asked me to press the Budget Committee, of which I was a member, to include funds for paving the road. A stretch of the uphill road was slippery and dangerous, as well as time-consuming.

The President of the Budget Committee was my fellow MP from Famagusta, Panagiotis Toumazis, who was reputed for his integrity and character. To include the Budget Committee request, there had to be a recommendation from the Ministry of Communications and Works.

I called Panayiotis Kazamias, the General Manager of Public Works with whom I had good friendly relations and raised the problem. He laughed.

"But how can I justify paving a road with a traffic load of 3 cars a day?"

After much discussion, he advised, "Tell them next Monday to mobilize local cars and other cars from the area to drive to Kellaki. I will install a meter from Public Works, and after the count, we will talk again." We did just what he advised. On Tuesday he called me.

"But Daphne," he said, "we were going to demonstrate more traffic, but how do we explain going from 5 cars crossing

[41]https://en.wikipedia.org/wiki/Northern_Cyprus_Water_Supply_Project

on previous days and then jumping to 48?"

But the figures were impressive, so the Kellaki road paving project was included in the budget, and the road was paved the following year.

RELOCATION OF KIVIDES VILLAGE

The relocation of Kivides is another case serving my constituents.

The village of Kato Kivides was built on clay soil, and every year the entire village was sliding downwards toward the riverbed. Houses collapsed, and there was a general sense of insecurity. The cost needed to move the village to a higher and safer point was beyond the State Budget's capabilities. However, under the guidance of the prolific teacher, Vyrona Byron, the inhabitants were persistent with their request to move their village to safer ground.

We thought to engage the House Speaker, Glafkos Clerides, with the issue.

I called Vyrona and informed him that the President of the House would be participating in the National Memorial Celebration for the fallen freedom fighters of Pachna village on the following Sunday. Following the Memorial, a big reception would take place. The House President, known for his fondness of Zivania[42], would take the opportunity to test the high-quality Zivania from Pachna.

On his way to Limassol after the celebration, when the president would be relaxed and laid back following his Zivania treat, it was an opportunity to warmly welcome him to Kivides to explain the need to move the village.

[42] https://en.wikipedia.org/wiki/Zivania

So, that is what happened. With arches, flags, and laurels, the entire community welcomed the House Speaker on his way back from Pachna. In his welcoming speech, Vyrona Byron raised the need to transfer the village to a safer place and asked the President to exercise his influence so that the move could occur.

In his reply, Clerides promised, in the enthusiastic atmosphere, that the request would be satisfied. The next day, the promise of the House President at Kivides was headline news.

It did not take long for the Minister of Finance to call me. 'But Mr. Daphne, do you, the MPs, and your President, think that we are printing money? What am I reading in the newspapers? His Beatitude called to tell me that we cannot leave the Kivides out of the Budget; it is something promised to its residents by the President of the House".

CREATING PAYROLL SUPER-SCALE

I was a member of the Budget Committee, the president being the Famagusta MP, the late Panagiotis Toumazis.

The President of the House of Representatives called for an extraordinary meeting of the Greek MPs. He announced His Beatitude's wish to create a new pay scale in the Government Payroll, which I described as a super-scale. The current pay scales were already much higher than the rankings of public servants we inherited from the English. At first, the president seemed reluctant to reveal why the House should approve the proposed super-scale. He then told us that His Beatitude had the wish to satisfy two of his close associates, Patroklos

Stavrou and Andreas Azinas. In return, the MPs' remuneration would increase from 92 pounds per month to 97.

I opposed both the creation of the super-scale and the increase in the remuneration of the MPs, arguing that the Government's salary was very satisfactory given the economic conditions prevailing at that time and that the pay of Members should only be for the purpose of representation. First, because the Members still maintain their normal incomes and jobs (mainly lawyers) and, as a result of their becoming MPs, their status had grown, and secondly, after all, an MP's position is not a livelihood job but a call to public service.

PROPOSING "INCOME AND WEALTH DISCLOSURE."

This proposed super scale prompted us, along with my Larnaca colleague MP Georgios Tzirkotis, to submit a bill to the House of Representatives requiring an "Income and Wealth Disclosure" from MPs and senior public employees. The bill had remained in the drawers of the House for over half a century. Recently, a law had been passed, a parody of what we proposed, leaving many loopholes, deliberately, I would say, to protect the full disclosure of the MPs' sources of enrichment.

ON THE SIDELINES OF THE LEGISLATIVE WORK

Cyprus, in the early 1960s, had had for me its sunny side too. Requests from both individuals and Communities were a daily routine.

The late priest of Agios Ioannis, Kyriakos Neophytos, had a vision that a huge river of oil was flowing under the village of Ypsonas at a great depth. It was still dark when he came to see me to report his discovery. He wanted me to immediately arrange an urgent meeting with Makarios to persuade him to begin drilling to extract this mineral wealth. Who knows, given the recent hydrocarbon discoveries, that Father Neophytos' dream was a prophetic revelation![43]

One evening, after voting on the first Poaching Law, I was late returning to Limassol when, close to the Agios Georgios Alamanos Monastery, a rabbit jumped in front of my car, got hit, and fell dead onto the asphalt. "Blessed be you, stupid," I said to myself. I felt sorry about this incident because after all, except for flies, mosquitoes, and cockroaches, I do not kill, and second, because I violated the law I had just voted for.

In order to have my conscience clear, I decided to inform the police of my transgression. I put the dead rabbit in the car and stopped at the Germasogeia police station. I spoke to the duty officer and told him he could use the rabbit as evidence if he wished (at his discretion).

On Sunday in the church of Kalo Chorio, Agia Marina, the church assistant, was Mr. Alcibiades, known as Arkis, whom Makarios also learned from his days as the Metropolitan Kition with Kalo Chorio under his jurisdiction.

Alcibiades was a known poacher, so much so that on his tomb in the Kalo Chorio cemetery, there is a rabbit trap!

"Give my greetings to Makarios," said Arkis, "and tell him to keep a close count on his animals, and when he finds any missing, to come to me to look for them." When I

[43]https://www.theguardian.com/world/2019/feb/28/huge-gas-discovery-offcyprus-could-boost-eu-energy-security

mentioned it to Makarios, he burst into laughter.

On another occasion, the then Limassol District Director, Christodoulos Benjamin, called me. "Mr. Daphne," he tells me, "We have a serious problem with Triantafyllides, the owner of the Rose Hotel. He blocked the police officers who wanted to investigate the hotel and insisted on talking to you in private to explain why." The Rose Hotel was close to "He roes Square," which then had a reputation for its cabarets and other nightclubs of shady repute.

I went to the office of Mr. Triantafyllides. After he closed the door, he told me that he did not want the police to enter the hotel's dressing room that day because they would have found a colleague of mine in a compromising situation, embarrassing the government of our Makarios!

POLITICAL MURDERS AND CRIMES

One of the darkest pages of the newly established Republic of Cyprus was the state of terror, the silencing of freedom of expression, provocative favoritism, and, worst of all, political murders. I mention this with a lot of pain because, in some cases, they were people murdered for their political beliefs.

On 16 August 1961, Neoclis Panagiotou and Euripides Nouros were murdered near the Moni Power Station while returning from Nicosia, where they had met the Interior minister Polykarpos Giorkatzis.

On 3 June 1973, Aristocles Avgoustis was assassinated at his farmhouse in Prastio Avdimou; he was an honest and decent EOKA fighter.

There were other cases that I am unable to ascertain. The disgrace of these murders is that there has been no attempt to detect and find those responsible. The names of the executioners were widely circulated, and some were even promoted to Public Service.

Along with the murders, there was systematic persecution of those considered to be "anti-Makarios." They were excluded from appointments to Public Service; they were not awarded scholarships and were persecuted with intimidation and in other ways.

An example of repressive measures and intimidation is the beating of the editor of the *Estia* Athens newspaper, Adonis Kyrou, by Christakis Tryfonides, who traveled to Athens for this purpose. Kyrou was a harsh critic of Makarios and the "Zurich Regime."[44]

Maybe the Mouflon,[45] which was the symbol of our bankrupt Cyprus Airways, is not related to the Zurich Constitution's collapse in December 1963, but the big ones are often learned from small transgressions.

During the transitional period toward Independence, the General Director of the Ministry of the Interior was Yiangos Antoniou, who, one morning, was visited in his office by Christakis Tryfonides, who asked him for permission to hunt mouflons in the Paphos forest. "It is forbidden to hunt mouflons; it is an endangered species. I am sorry I cannot give you the permit you are asking for."

---

[44] Estia (polytonic : Istia) is an Athenian afternoon political, cultural and economic newspaper published since 1876. As for politics and culture, it can be classified as a conservative newspaper.
[45] https://www.cyprusalive.com/en/cyprus-mouflon-ovis-orientalis-ophion

"But you know who you're talking to? Tomorrow you will be sorry!" The following day, Tryfonides returned with a note from Makarios with his famous signature in red ink.

"You are ordered to issue permission to the bearer of this note to hunt mouflons."

Instead of answering, Yiangos Antoniou handed Tryfonides his letter to Makarios in which he submitted his resignation. "Give my greetings to the Archbishop, and I wish good luck to the State that he is creating."

Sadly, Yiangos Antoniou's wish for good luck for the new Republic was not to be fulfilled.

I RESIGN FROM THE HOUSE OF REPRESENTATIVES AND LEAVE FOR THE UNITED STATES

In 1966 I decided to resign from the Cyprus House of Representatives to travel to the United States for the opportunity to attend University since, when at an earlier time, I could have attended, I was the "guest" of Queen Elizabeth in Omorphita and Kokkinotrimithia Detention Camps!

CHAPTER FIVE

EVENTS AFTER MY SERVICE
AT THE HOUSE OF REPRESENTATIVES

I traveled to the united states on a state department observation visit when I visited my brother, a graduate student at Iowa State University in 1966. At the end of that official visit, I enrolled at Iowa State University as a first-year student.

HOW I ACCESSED A CONFIDENTIAL STATE DEPARTMENT REPORT ON CYPRUS

One morning in March 1969, my academic advisor and coach, John Timmons, invited me to his office. "I would like you to become vice president of our Institute of International Affairs."

John Timmons had a keen interest in international affairs. He had just presented Robert Parks, the President of the University, with his report entitled "The Role of the University in the International Community." He believed that the United States had to contribute to global economic development actively. He systematically worked on developing agrarian reform programs in Vietnam, Peru, and other Third World countries.

The President of the Institute of International Affairs was the Head of the School of English Literature, Professor Laurie. He was a short, brave man with a sense of humor, very accessible, and lovable. He explained to me that the purpose of the Institute was to sensitize the University community as well as the rural, isolated population of the State of Iowa, to major global problems such as Hunger, the Cold War, the Palestinian/Israeli Conflict, Racial Conflict, Vietnam, Petroleum, all of which stood out. Each year, we would pick a problem and organize seminars, workshops, exhibitions, and radio and TV shows regarding the academic year's selected issue. As a culmination of these activities, we invited a wellknown personality to discuss the chosen problem with the University Community in the Spring in-depth.

Having discussed the selection for a long time, we agreed to propose the Palestinian/Israeli Conflict as the theme of the year and have Dankwart A. Rustow, a Professor at Columbia University and State Department Advisor, as the speaker.

The University Administration accepted the Institute's choice of the Palestinian issue. So in the spring of 1970, we had with us Professor Dankwart A. Rustow for a few days on campus. I was the Vice President of the Institute at that time. I noticed that Professor Rostow's CV contained, among other things, that he was also the author of a study on Cyprus: "The Cyprus Conflict and United States Security Interests." The RAND Corporation conducted the study on behalf of the U.S. Department of Defense and aimed at defining the United States foreign policy towards its two allies in NATO, Greece and Turkey. RAND Corporation was regarded by many as a CIA branch, with which it maintained close cooperation.

I undertook to accompany Professor Rustow during his stay, so I could discuss many aspects of the Cyprus problem. I asked him if he would send me a copy of his Cyprus study, which he offered with much courtesy to do. "Call Mary Keith," he told me, "and tell her to send you the study." I was very anxious to know how the Americans saw our problem after Makarios rejected the American-inspired Acheson Plan. I was disappointed when Mrs. Keith informed me that the Report was a confidential document and that it was impossible to send it to me. This made me want to see what the study was saying even more.

There was a lot of talk about Murphy's Law in those days. All the economics and business administration students and the students of psychology and sociology are familiar with Murphy's Law, which, simply put, says, "If something can go wrong, it will soon go wrong."

I decided to test this Law. "Maybe," I told myself, "if I insist, repeating my request many times, something may give in and allow my access to the confidential report."

The Department of Economics had just received the latest model of a Xerox photocopier for the office. It was one of the first copiers to automatically make multiple copies. It was three meters long, making an unusual whining sound while processing the copies. I embarked on writing a letter to the RAND Corporation Headquarters in Santa Monica, California, asking for the report for which I had the author's consent. I insisted on repeating my request, mailing one every Monday, having made 15 copies of my letter for this purpose. I kept getting the same standard answer from Rand. "The report 'RM-5416-ISA (FOUO), The Cyprus Conflict and the United States Security Interests,' was not releasable."

To my great surprise, after the seventh of my requests,

I found in my mailbox the Report itself! I read it carefully, two to three times, and each time the red underlining rang on each page. This is one of the few cases in my life that I did not follow up with a "thank you" to a person for giving me such an important present.

The report makes a snapshot analysis of the problem first and notes that the failure to find a viable solution was because negotiations took place between Athens and Ankara, while the solution mainly concerned Cyprus.

The report analyzed the implications for the security of the United States from three scenarios.

1. Thermonuclear war between America and the Soviet Union,

2. Limited Soviet military intervention in the Mediterranean, the Middle East, and Africa,

3. Limited-scale military operations in the same region and South Asia on behalf of the West.

While the study highlighted the importance for both the United States and NATO of the good relations between Greece and Turkey and the need for the United States to do everything in its power to keep the balance between these two allies, I considered the essence of American policy as far as Cyprus was concerned. "If," concluded the study, "once the United States finds itself in the dilemma of choosing between Greece and Turkey, the interests of the United States are closing the bulwark in favor of Turkey."

I did not waste time; I immediately sent it to Makarios.

135

He was impressed, and he had wrongly made the impression that I had access to the American Government's top strata. This comes from two examples. After the first letter I sent to him, in his reply, he asked me if I could provide him with other such reports, and later, when he was persecuted by the coup in July 1974, he came to Washington and stayed for a few days at the home of the Ambassador of Cyprus, Nikos Demetriou. I was then also in Washington at the home of my brother, Stahis, and sister-in-law, Joy, on my way to Cyprus, where I had accepted the position as the General Manager of the Fasouri Plantation. I made the decision not to change my plans regardless of the invasion. My family would stay in the U.S. until the situation was normalized. While in this position, I would be managing the largest Cyprus plantation, contributing to strengthening citrus growing, an important export product for the Cypriot economy. Traditionally the most important orchards were in Morphou, Famagusta, and Lefka, which were already in Turkish-occupied areas. Thus, the government's interest turned to the few but essential citrus fruit plantations in the area west of Limassol.[46]

I was visiting my brother at his office in the World Bank when Nikos Demetriou, the Cyprus Ambassador to the United States, called, saying, "His Holiness wants to see you in my home." We went with my brother, a good friend of the Ambassador, to the Residence. The Archbishop was on the upper floor while in the living room, besides the Ambassador,

[46]During his stay, the two of us brothers went out for lunch one day to discuss the Fasouri Plantation job its pros and cons, and the questions he should raise with the owners when Dafnis was to arrive in Cyprus.

We both had studied decision theory in our applied economics courses and we now had a case to apply it.

We applied a simple model by defining two columns, one with pluses and the other with the negatives. The Positives were a good salary and benefits, including a house, the contribution to the economy at this critical time, his applying his cutting edge of agronomic knowledge, and more. On the negative side, the main concern was the disruption of the family which was very well adapted to the life, work and school in the University town of Ames, Iowa. In his case, he would be abandoning his PhD work expecting it to be finished in a couple of months.

Dafnis stayed in Cyprus for a week, and upon his return, I drove to Dulles airport to meet him. As we were driving in my Peugeot 304, I waited to hear his decision about Fassouri and if our "decision theory" analysis was helpful. Dafnis, in his characteristic agreeable conversational style, recounted his arrival in Cyprus and his sadness due to the devastation caused by the Turkish invasion, the destruction and the thousands of the displaced people, now refugees in their own land. "Dafnis," I interrupted, "and your decision for the job?"

Dafnis paused for a second and said: "I accepted the job, but we left out our decision model, a most important variable." He went on describing his arrival at the Plantation with the miles of road lined with tall cypress trees on both sides, and many acres of orange trees and grape vines. And then the house, next to a pond, covered with the most beautiful bougainvillea. "At that moment," he said, "I made my decision on the spot to accept the job!"

*The lesson from this experience is to remind us that in life's decisions there is, at times hidden, **"the bougainvillea factor".***

was Giorgos Pelagias, the Deputy Foreign Minister and a close and trusted associate of Makarios and Andros Nicolaides, a Cyprus diplomat and former EOKA member.

I went upstairs alone. The Archbishop was sitting on the couch, and I greeted him in the Greek Orthodox tradition, kissing his hand, and began to refer to news from Cyprus. Makarios went straight to why he asked to see me.

"I know that you have close relationships with the State Department. I want you to ask them to tell you candidly what requirements and what terms they want to facilitate my return to Cyprus."

"Your Holiness," I replied, "I have no access to the State Department. I just have two friends who had served in Cyprus when I was a Member of the House of Representatives. One of them is now at the State Department under Henry Kissinger."

I referred to Charles W. McCaskill[47], who oversaw the Cyprus Desk Office; I also knew Tom Boyat, Frank Jones, and Dick Wells.

When I arrived at McCaskill's office, I found him watching live TV that, at that moment, was showing black smoke covering Famagusta and the landing of Turkish paratroopers.

We embraced, crying together for several minutes. "Dafnis, these sad moments should have been avoided, never to have happened."

"Yes," I said, "but let us see where we go from now on."

"Makarios is in Washington; did you see him?" he asked.

I gave him Makarios' message.

---

[47]http://www.helleniccomserve.com/charleswmccaskillsr.html

"Cyprus is very unlucky at this time," McCaskill told me. "We, Americans, are in one of the most serious political crises in the history of America. I do not think we can do much these days. The Secretary is in California with President Nixon. There is essentially no government in Washington. I will forward Makarios' request to the Secretary, so come back tomorrow morning for coffee when I expect to have heard from him."

The political crisis from the Watergate scandal was at its peak. [48]At any moment, Congress was expected to vote for President Nixon's impeachment, who was at this time at a California farm with his close associates debating how to address the political crisis.

I informed Makarios, and we waited until the next morning to hear from Kissinger, whose answer to Makarios' plea was frosty and characteristic of his arrogant style.

"Let things take their course," he told McCaskill. Any hope for American intervention to halt the Turkish invasion, as was done in 1964 when President Lyndon Johnson was President, was not going to happen.[49] For Kissinger, who never had a good opinion about Makarios, it was time to avenge "the Fidel Castro of the Mediterranean."

McCaskill's attempts to positively influence his political chief 's opinion in favor of the Greek Cypriots fell into a

---

[48]https://en.wikipedia.org/wiki/Watergate_scandal
[49]The New York Times: JOHNSON WARNS INONU ON CYPRUS Invites Him to U.S. for Talks — Turkey Said to Give Up Plan for a Landing WASHINGTON, June 5 [1964]—President Johnson has moved to head off further inflammation of the Cyprus crisis by cautioning Turkey against any rash military moves and inviting the Turkish Premier, Ismet Inonu, here for discussions.

vacuum. It was too late for Makarios to offer anything to the West. The whole of North Cyprus could now be a NATO base without his consent.

In comparison, the Acheson Plan was rejected by Makarios 10 years earlier under the pressure of Soviet allied AKEL, and his doctor Vasos Lyssaridis[50] offered a Turkish base with just 178 soldiers in Karpasia.[51] With Makarios at the helm, Cyprus continued to be a proud member of the Non-Allied Nations, which had neither the power nor the political will to assist Cyprus in this hour of need. Nor did help come during these tragic 1974 moments from other allies such as Egypt, the Soviet Union, and Yugoslavia.

As I got up to leave, McCaskill asked me to stay a few more minutes. He took a note from the desk drawer and said: "Give these names to Makarios and ask him if he is willing to return to Cyprus to form a government with this composition."

I took a quick look at the note on which there was a list of recommended names. Glafcos Clerides was at the head, followed by Andonis Anastasiadis, Emilios Frangos, Pavlos Pavlakis, and Andreas Araouzou. To please me, my name was included in the list.

I gave Makarios a detailed account of my conversation with Charles McCaskill and gave him the note with the names. I was astounded when he pulled a pen from his robes and drew a red line on one of the names declaring, "this one, no!" It was Pavlos Pavlakis, the well-known entrepreneur of Famagusta. I was surprised by this rejection, as I knew the integrity of Pavlos Pavlakis and his cooperation with

---

[50]https://en.wikipedia.org/wiki/Vassos_Lyssarides
[51]See Annex the Dean Acheson letter of 20th of August 1964, to Prime Minister Papandreou.

Makarios in the early years of Cyprus' Independence. I later learned from Andros Nicolaides that the brother-in-law and partner of Pavlakis, Kikis, was part of a failed assassination attempt against Makarios near the village of Ag Sergios.

The next day I left Washington for Cyprus.

THE ACHESON PLAN

In the summer of 1964, there were strong rumors that after an American intervention with Turkey's consent, the Union of Cyprus and Greece was underway. This news was not just rumors. The Greek Prime Minister, George Papandreou, whom I saw with other colleagues of the Cyprus House of Representatives, informed us that he asked the members of the Greek House of Representatives to be standing by, ready to return to Athens to attend the historic meeting ratifying the union of Cyprus with Greece. Everyone was anxiously waiting for Archbishop Makarios' approval of the plan known as the Acheson Plan. The Greek Foreign Minister, Petros Garoufalias, had traveled to Cyprus to persuade Makarios to accept the plan.

I was in the Cyprus House of Representatives Building at a meeting of the Budget Committee chaired by Panagiotis Toumasis, when the House's telephone operator, Mrs. Paraskevas Lazaris, told me that the American Ambassador, Taylor Belcher, urgently wanted to talk to me.

I called him. "Come to my office right away," he said, "I need you for something urgent."

"You have good relations with the General [Grivas]," he said. "What does he think of the Acheson Plan? Has he instructed his followers for their stand?"

"Toby," I said, "apart from what we read in the newspapers, neither Digenis nor Makarios nor the Speaker of the House has informed us on this matter."

"I have reserved a place on the flight to Athens for you to consult with Grivas," and he handed me the ticket.

I went straight from Athens Airport to Grivas' home. Many people were there waiting to meet with Digenis, who at the time had announced his intention, a wrong one, in my opinion, to enter the political arena in Greece. I joined the others waiting for my turn when Dimitris Filiastides, Grivas' Office Manager, noticed me in the waiting lounge. I had hosted Philiastides for a few days at my house when he was wanted by the British following an EOKA ambush of British Forces in Larnaca. He informed Digenis that I was waiting outside. Leaving his office and his other guests, he immediately came out to meet me.

"Well," he greeted me with his familiar accent, "what are you doing here?"

"Chief, we're completely in the dark about the Acheson Plan. The fighters want to know your views. Do we accept it or reject it?" I said, without revealing the exact reason for my visit!

Grivas: "How can I answer you? No one showed me the Plan, and I don't know more than what you read in the newspapers."

"How is it possible that such an important document has not been communicated to you by either Cyprus or Athens or the Americans?" I asked.

Grivas: "Do you understand what I'm saying, or have you

too become a politician? No one, no one, has communicated with me. They rip and sew as they please. But listen, my dear Dafnis, the Communists rule in Cyprus. Ask Papaioannou, who is also your colleague in the House of Representatives. That's whom Makarios will also ask."[52]

I returned to Cyprus the next day and informed the American Ambassador. He was surprised. He was under the impression that the Greek Government had informed Digenis.

"By tonight," he told me, "you'll have the Plan in your hands."

But it was too late. Leaving Ambassador Belcher's office, I was informed that Makarios had rejected the Acheson Plan. "The only acceptable solution for the Cypriot people," he said, "was a genuine Union, without a NATO base, and with the closure of the British Bases."

(See the documents of the Acheson Plan in the ANNEX FIVE)

A TEMPTING PROPOSAL FROM THE CIA

It was January 1974, and I was working on my doctoral thesis in my office at Iowa State University when I received a call from the Dean of the Department of Economics, Dr. Raymond Beneke. Dr. Beneke was very much appreciated for his honesty and ethos, and my relationship with him was one of friendship and trust.

"Daphne," he told me, "two gentlemen from the CIA came from Chicago asking for information about you. They

---

[52] https://en.wikipedia.org/wiki/Ezekias_Papaioannou

are interested in knowing who is funding your studies and how you support your family with a wife and four children. I referred them to your office 104. Do you accept them?"

"Why not? Invite them to my office," I replied.

Soon, two tall gentlemen knocked on my office door. They were both wearing black raincoats and dark glasses, reminding me of characters out of crime and espionage movies.

The two introduced themselves and gave me their cards. They were CIA officials seconded to the Chicago office, which was responsible for America's midwestern states. It was approaching noon, and I invited them for lunch, which they accepted.

Without much delay, we addressed the reason for their visit. "Yes, I have a big family. My wife works as a cleaning lady at the Holiday Inn. And to make ends meet, I work at a $3.75-an-hour part-time job at Metal Products in addition to my services as a consultant in the Foreign Student Office. I also teach for four hours a week."

"Are you thinking of being active politically upon your return to Cyprus?"

"Interest in service for the common good is an obligation in democratic states. That is what the Ancient Greeks bequeathed to us," I returned.

"We are interested in employing you as an agro-economic field analyst."

They proceeded to offer me incredibly attractive terms of employment, and after thanking them, I replied that the proposal interested me. They gave me a ticket to travel to Washington to discuss the details and sign the CIA employment contract. They were booking a room for me at the Holiday Inn in the Washington suburb of Virginia, somewhere near the CIA Headquarters in Langley.

I informed them that I preferred to stay with my brother, who worked at the World Bank, and lived in Bethesda. There was no need for a hotel reservation. I thanked them for lunch and left the restaurant.

At the meeting in Washington two days later, I was met by a gentleman who came on behalf of the Service and introduced himself as George, of Greek origin. We went through the contract article-by-article and agreed on everything.

He then handed me a document and said, "Before you sign the contract, you must sign this statement."

The document was a typed text in which I would declare allegiance to the American Constitution and that my work would serve the United States' interests.

"George, I cannot sign this," I said. "I have taken an oath of allegiance to the Constitution of Cyprus as a citizen of the Republic of Cyprus."

He tried to change my mind, disappointed when he realized that he could not change my position. In closing his briefcase, he conveyed to me with a dose of irony: "You'd be surprised to know how many of your friends have signed this statement."

Did I decline a profitable opportunity?

It has been many years since. As I write these lines describing the lost opportunity to be a CIA agent, I am on a list of unwanted persons prohibited from entering the United States. The FBI finds me to be dangerous to the security of the United States!

Could it be that in having me on the unwelcome list, the culprit is the outcome of my CIA encounter? I cannot say for sure or if I should laugh or cry.

IS THERE HOPE?

I do not think that we can soon hope for a drastic change in our island's unhappy results to where our chosen policies brought us. But let us not give up hope, recalling the wise Heraclitus maxim, "πάντα ρεῖ," "everything flows." ["Nothing stays the same."] Things that are in our imaginations now, impossible, may take place in the future. Since the fall of Constantinople to the Ottoman Turks on May 29, 1453, we Greeks have been in the wishful stage, dreaming of our return. It is time for us Greek Cypriots to give up wishful ideal solutions for Cyprus instead of accepting work for a functional and sustainable solution to our problem.

To have a chance of leaving the stalemate we are now in; however, certain conditions must be fulfilled:

- Admit the mistakes we made,

- Harness the enormous human resources that we have worldwide,

- Redefine our objectives as dictated by the geopolitical conditions of our region.

CAESAROPAPISM IN CYPRUS AND ITS CONSEQUENCES

The absence of a normal policy-instituting tradition in Cyprus is due to the survival of the Ethnarchy institution. An institution bequeathed to us over the centuries of Ottoman rule.

Vasilis Michaelides, in his memorable poem "July 1821", describes the visit of Turkish Cypriot Kioroglou to Archbishop Kyprianos to persuade him to take him to the diplomatic homes in Larnaca to avoid his hanging that the Ottomans were planning at the dawn of the next day, thereby thwarting any attempt of the Cypriots joining the 1821 Greek uprising.

When a leader gathers both political and ecclesiastical power in his person, we have the phenomenon of Caesaropapism. The institution of Caesaropapism was practiced in the Middle Ages by the Catholic West, unlike the Orthodox East, where often the Church opposed the Emperor.

The Bishop-Writer-Professor at Cambridge, UK, Kallistos Ware, in his book "The Orthodox Way", presents Cyprus as the only recent case with the revival of the medieval institution of Caesaropapism, where the President [Makarios] combined the power of a secular government with religious authority. This explains why, for the Greek Cypriots, Makarios was "the One and only One." Even Grivas, when announcing the end of EOKA, ordered absolute discipline to the "One," i.e., to Makarios.

Sadly, those days of unity soon ended when the calamity of the division made its appearance. Makarios and Grivas led the people into a confrontation between "pro- Makarios" and "pro-Grivas" forces.

During a brief visit from the United States to Cyprus,

when EOKA B was at its peak, I asked Grivas if his purpose was to overthrow Makarios.

"Listen, son," he said in a sad tone. "Stay where you are because this place will be destroyed. As far as Makarios is concerned, they press me to permit them to eliminate him, but I will not murder one who wears a priestly robe. But if you see him, say hello to him on my behalf and tell him that I beg him to take his Holy Water and go to his church."

Makarios' dual-status also predetermined the fate of the State of which he was President. He must have had a problem with a divisive personality. In the church, he was the Orthodox Archbishop and the "Ethnarch" of Cypriot Hellenism. At the Presidential Palace, he was the President of (the secular) State, of which 18% were Turkish Cypriot Muslims. Three of them were members of the Cabinet, and all three were high-ranking officials of the Turkish organization, TMT.

It is also worth recalling that the supposedly "Progressive Left" did not object seriously to Makarios Caesaropapism. In the 1968 presidential elections, Psychiatrist Takis Evdokas opposed Makarios, receiving only 3.74% of the vote. For his speaking out against Government abuses, he ended up in Central Prison!

Characteristic were the comments that prevailed then, mostly in the villages. An aunt of mine could not understand how someone who was not even ordained, such as Evdokas, wanted to be President of Cyprus! Makarios was the genuine representative of the charismatic personality described by the German sociologist Max Weber.

As an example of this, Charles Foley (the journalist) told me in a personal conversation that Makarios invited him to visit mountainous Spilia together on a Sunday. Makarios was greeted with flags, laurels, slogans, and cheers. At that moment, His Beatitude proudly whispered in Foley's ear, "See what I can do if I move my finger?"

CONCLUDING OBSERVATIONS

The Cyprus issue began to be projected into the International Spotlight after the Second World War, as a request for Union with Greece, at the beginning, and as a request for "Self-Determination and Union" developing into a "Demand for Independence," to end up as an unprecedented and unsustainable form of an independent state.

The Constitution of the Republic of Cyprus that came out of the signing of the Zurich-London Agreements is a "tragic and in many cases almost ridiculously absurd text," as characterized by the Constitutional Law Professor Stanley De Smith.

The study of history is necessary in order not to repeat the same mistakes. From being taught by past mistakes, history is mainly shaped by leaders who often have no vision, nor the needed selflessness or self-denial. Few leaders in history have been found to possess these characteristics (Pericles, Marcus Aurelius, Lincoln, Churchill). In Cyprus's case, at the critical historical juncture of the end of the Second World War, neither in Cyprus nor Greece were we fortunate enough to have such leaders.

Cyprus's struggle was conducted with national and religious sentimentality as if Cyprus were something unrelated to all these developments. And that is not all! We came to the point of believing that we, like Cyprus, could play a decisive role in shaping the major powers' politics!

… "the Bridge between East and West," proclaimed Makarios that he intended to make of Cyprus… a "Nation of Progress, a Nation of Prosperity a Nation of God," apparently bearing in mind the Theocentric State of Saint Augustine.

The fratricide of Cyprus Hellenism resulting from Makarios and Grivas' animosity and personal ambitions sealed the Cyprus Republic's collapse and fashioned the road for the 1974 Turkey invasion.

An effort to reconcile Makarios with Digenis was made by Doctor Marios Tritoftides, recommending Makarios's resignation from the Presidency of the Republic of Cyprus and the appointment of a person of common acceptance, a suggestion made by General Grivas in a letter to Makarios.

Makarios promised to reply in three weeks at the most. Grivas never got an answer. Any hope of national reconciliation had evaporated. The events that followed by the intensification of EOKA B's actions on the one hand, and the abuses of government forces and parastate groups on the other, sealed the demise of the Cyprus Republic, questioning the confidençe and identity of Cyprus Hellenism.

At that time, I was in the United States and read the Cypriot newspapers' cryptic headlines. "We gained ground," they wrote, every time we got a favorable vote. I did not see anything bright, and I was concerned that Makarios and his advisers believed that the resolutions that were in our favor with the support of the Non-aligned Countries would actually bring us closer to the solution. I wrote to my friend and best man, Yannis Papadopoulos, a distinguished writer and poet and an active member of EOKA, to give me his own impartial opinion. His answer was brief and typical: "The only ground we gained," the late Yiannis wrote, "are the two meters of filling extending the Limassol waterfront."

When, after the crisis that erupted with the Turkish mutiny in December 1963, missions were sent to enlighten foreign governments of the soundness of our policies. Makarios told us: "I will go personally to Africa. I will impress them with my robes and beard!"

He was usually accompanied by the Minister of Foreign Affairs and, later, the President of the Republic, Spyros Kyprianou. Once when Makarios was in Germany as an official guest of Adenauer, an employee of the German Ministry of Foreign Affairs (of Armenian origin) who was present at that dinner and who later moved to Cyprus, invited me for dinner at his home in Vouni to thank me for giving his daughter some stamps for her collection. He related that at the official German dinner offered to Makarios and the political leaders from Africa, one of the African guests asked him if Orthodox High Priests could marry and have a family. That was when he saw an African pointing his finger toward the Cypriot Foreign Minister and asked Makarios: "Your Majesty, is this little kid your son? I have 18. How many kids do you have?"

"I did not hear the Cypriot President's reply."

At a conference of the Non-aligned Countries in Bandu, as Makarios himself told us, Prime Minister Nehru of India, after congratulating him on his Presidency, advised him on four things:

"Your Grace," Nehru advised, "do not make the mistakes we made:

a) Stay in the Commonwealth, b) Keep the English language, c) Safeguard Civil Service that you inherited from the English, and d) Safeguard your Judiciary as well."

When we were asked to join the British Commonwealth,

Glafkos Clerides, at the behest of Makarios, invited to his office those who came from the ranks of EOKA and urged us to vote in favor of membership, so the decision of the House would be unanimous. For us who had fought against British colonial rule, this was a matter of conscience. We stood up, Pavlos Pavlakis, Kostas Christodoulides, Dafni Panagides, Giannakis Giamakis, and Nikos Angelidis and voted against joining the British Commonwealth. This displeased the Archbishop. If joining the Commonwealth has yielded political or other benefits for Cyprus, it is not the subject of this writing at this time.

WHY WE ARE WHERE WE ARE

As mentioned above, the most decisive factors in the historical course of Cyprus after the Second World War were:

- The absence of a political leader,

- The use of armed violence as a means of freeing ourselves from the colonial yoke,

- The rejection of the West and our accession to the Group of Nonaligned Countries,

- The under-estimation of Turkey's role in the region,

- The cold-war climate of the time, and

- Serious deficits in the management of the Zurich Constitution.

Let us look at some of these factors in more detail.

THE ABSENSE OF A POLITICAL LEADER

During the critical years reviewed in this book, Cyprus Hellenism's fortunes were, in Cyprus, in the hands of the Church and, in Greece, in the hands of the military. But, unfortunately for Cyprus, neither the military schools nor the cells of Monasteries are designed to produce political leaders who can understand and manage intricate diplomatic problems, especially the ones of the Eastern Mediterranean created by the post-war period and the Cold War.

To Epimarchos, a philosopher of the ⁵th century BC from the island of Kos is attributed the maxim «Ου μετανοείν αλλά προνοείν χρη τον άνδρα τον σοφόν,» "The wise man anticipates so as not having to regret in hindsight."

An Intelligence Service official whom I met by chance in Saudi Arabia (he had since retired) was working for the British Ministry of Defense to supply weapon systems to Saudi Arabia. He told me that when he was serving in Cyprus, spying on me was one of his tasks. We became friends. In a report by the Intelligence Service to the Ministry of Defense on Makarios' personality, Makarios was described as "very intelligent but not wise."

Of course, we did not have a history of free democratic life, unlike Turkey, which had a long history of political activity. In Greece, the "upper hand" was held by the military even before the dictatorship years when General Papagos was Prime Minister.

ANTI-WESTERN ORIENTATION

The frustration and disappointment of the Cypriot people with the outcome of the Struggle, due, to a great extent, to the role of the West, especially Great Britain, explains Makarios' decision to integrate Cyprus into the Coalition of Non-Aligned States in 1962. We, from the ranks of EOKA, too, felt deeply disappointed with the West.

The study of behind-the-scenes actions that led to Zurich leaves no doubt that the main rationale for the settlement of the Cyprus issue was not a matter of justice for a struggling people but the safeguarding of the interests of Europe and America, with NATO as their main representative. All the members involved, Greece, Turkey, and England, were members of the North Atlantic Alliance, so it was considered natural that Cyprus would remain in the same "family." From the moment Makarios turned his back on the Western World, the countdown began for Cyprus. All of the projects proposed a solution to the Cyprus issue before and after Zurich, such as the British proposals, the Acheson Project, the Annan Project, and the Bi-Communal Bi-Zonal Federation were intended to serve the geostrategic plans of NATO countries.

This intense anti-Western feeling of the Cypriots because of the liberation struggle's unfulfilled expectations was taken advantage of by pro Soviet AKEL. With Makarios a close partner, Cyprus turned away from the West. With his ambitious nature, Makarios saw the Non-Aligned countries as a platform for him to play an important role internationally. And indeed, Makarios did play an important role in the Non-Aligned Movement. Many resolutions favorable to Cyprus voted at the United Nations were the results of Makarios' prestige in the countries of the Third World of Africa and Asia.

We opted to invest our political and national future in Eastern Europe and the Third World countries. It is no coincidence that we are bankrupt today as those we had invested in have also gone bankrupt! The political alliance of the Church and Communist AKEL helped us collect many favorable UN resolutions. Unfortunately, it did not prevent Turkey from invading and occupying 36% of Cyprus for almost 50 years.

THE USE OF ARMED VIOLENCE AS THE MEANS OF EXPELLING THE COLONIAL YOKE.

The original intention of our struggle for freedom was to "create noise" with a few explosions for people to know that Cyprus existed. But things did not stay that way. The armed struggle expanded, and while it was given a lot of publicity internationally, at the same time, it rekindled Turkish nationalism leading to a consequential ethnic conflict. It also cultivated feelings of hostility against us in Great Britain and the West, discounting diplomacy and flexibility in our pursuit of self-determination. The sense of national pride and patriotic fulfillment that the selfsacrifice and heroic feats of the freedom fighters cultivated for Greeks everywhere were insufficient to fulfill our expectations.

CHAPTER SIX

REFLECTIONS

The chapters up to here are a narrative description of the background of the recent history of Cyprus. However, the study of history without reflection and, above all, without becoming a beacon of guidance for the future remains a dull recounting of events - either to unleash nationalist wisdom or evoke feelings of pessimism or defeatism. We live the consequences of the events that we described in the previous chapters.

As the great Socrates stated in his Apology, "The unexamined life is not worth living" (ὁ δὲ ἀνεξέταστος βίος οὐ βιωτὸς ἀνθρώπῳ). Indeed, an analysis of the historical facts is needed - difficult as that may be.

THE "IF" IN THE ANALYSIS OF HISTORICAL EVENTS

One of the most talked-about theories in historiography is the theory of "If." It is an attempt to analyze historical events by projecting an opposite historical scenario from what took place. For example, we can ask the question:

- "What would the world be like today if the Soviet Bloc hadn't collapsed?"

In the same way, we can create countless scenarios by raising questions such as:

- "What would things be like today if we had accepted the British Radcliffe proposals or the Acheson Plan?" or

- "What if Makarios chose NATO instead of the third World NonAligned?" or

- "What if the 1974 Coup didn't happen?"…, and so on.

The American philosopher, Sidney Hook, rejects this approach because the historical event is the real thing, while the "ifs" are constructs from the imagination. These are scenarios that are not scientifically documented. Apart from what took place, the possible scenarios cannot be precisely defined for the historical analyst to substantiate.

However, a variety of scenarios have been examined concerning the Cyprus problem. They are usually divided into two categories, "pro-western" scenarios and "anti-western" orientation scenarios. All we must do is look at some of the book titles written from the 1960s onward.

But I agree with Sidney Hook's view that the "if" theoretical approach puts a barrier to creative thinking and excludes broader and more transparent historical research. I would say that a better research tool is the analysis of history based on the mathematical formulas of probabilities. We can study different scenarios with different possibilities[53].

For example, the researcher may assume that the possibility of a

Turkish invasion in the event of a Coup d'Etat, is 0.99, while the possibility of intervention from outer space is zero. The result would vindicate the historical investigator as the assumptions made are consistent with what happened.

One of Makarios' first biographers was an employee of the Cyprus Diplomatic Service. I asked him if he learned how Makarios made the big and serious decisions of his political career. He said he once asked Makarios how he dealt with big and difficult decisions.

"I decide without delay," was his reply. "Then I have time to study the decision!"

It is accepted that history is necessary to help us not repeat the same mistakes. But that is not what we see happening. Quite the opposite, we repeat the same mistakes of the past. Political leaders shape history, and regrettably, leaders rarely showed vision, selflessness, or commitment to the common good. In our case, at the critical historical junctures following the Second World War, neither in Cyprus nor in Greece were we fortunate to have better leaders.

Historical events must be examined in the setting and circumstances in which they took place. The geopolitical circumstances that prevailed after the Second World War, plus how the political leadership in Cyprus and Greece managed Cyprus's fate concerning these circumstances, were decisive factors in our modern Cypriot history. Unfortunately, both Cyprus and Greece's political leadership did not take these significant decisive factors into account in their support of

_____

[53]https://en.wikipedia.org/wiki/Sidney_Hook

Cyprus' independence.

A cultural characteristic of the Greeks, and more so Greek Cypriots, due to being invaded by outsiders throughout our history, is to blame others for our problems; there is always a scapegoat. We transfer responsibilities to third parties, absolving ourselves for any wrongdoing, keeping our consciences clear. We have discovered a lot of such goats in our recent history. Depending on our ideological positions, our calamity's responsibility lies with the Anglo-Americans, the CIA, Europe, Imperialism, Communism, AKEL, Makarios, Grivas. What about our role? We had no part in what happened? We are innocent on all fronts?

POSSIBLE SOLUTIONS

I now come to a brief evaluation of the scenarios being put forward as possible solutions to the long-standing Cyprus problem.

If the armed struggle aimed to give us heroes to honor and immortalize, we could say that the armed struggle was a great success. A visit to the graves of the executed EOKA fighters in Nicosia's central prison fills the visitor with reverence and patriotic admiration.[54]

If, on the other hand, we evaluate what we accomplished

[54]The "Imprisoned Graves" are a set of graves in a small cemetery located in the Central Jail of Nicosia, where 13 EOKA fighters, during the 1955–1959 liberation struggle for the liberation of Cyprus from the United Kingdom, were interred. Nine of them were hanged. The tombs were built in an area adjacent to the cells of the condemned and close to the gallows where they were executed. The area is surrounded by tall walls and covered by glass. Having a small, private cemetery was the idea of Cyprus Governor Sir John Harding, who did not want the funerals of EOKA fighters to be turned into demonstrations against British rule. The condemned, as well as the four others who died, will have been buried in that area without any relatives or priests present. The nine men who were hanged were buried immediately following their executions. To save space, they were buried two to a grave. After Cyprus gained her independence, the area became a national monument, where thousands visit. A sign from Greek heroic history is carved into the wall reminding that "Του ανδρειωμένου ο θάνατος, θάνατος δεν λογιέται" - "The brave man's death is not to be thought of as death at all." https://en.wikipedia.org/wiki/Imprisoned_Graves

of the central aim of the struggle - the Union with Mother Greece, the armed struggle was undeniably a disastrous failure. Before the decisive battle in Waterloo, Napoleon's generals reassured him that France would win because he had God on her side. Napoleon replied, "Unfortunately, God is with those who have the most cannons."

The excruciating question for us is whether a solution of the BiZonal Bi-Communal Federation (BBF), which UN resolutions embrace as desirable, is workable. Unfortunately, it is, in my view, worse than the failed Zurich Agreements.[55] If such an arrangement is reached, which I doubt will happen, we will pay a heavy price for another painful experiment.

The geopolitical conditions that shaped the Zurich solution remain. Indeed, they have become tougher constraints. While the Soviet bloc has disbanded, the U.S. and Europe's confrontation with Russia remains. Instability and severe conflicts in the region [Syria, Libya. Iraq, Yemen], with the discovery of important gas deposits, has made finding a solution more difficult. [56]Simultaneously, the rise of extremist Islam has upgraded Turkey's role. In such an environment, how can we win?

At the time when conditions were more favorable, we chose our own uncertain paths. Let us now attempt a brief evaluation of the scenarios which are put forward as possible solutions.

---

[55] The Bi-Zonal Bi-Communal Federation (BBF), a settlement with political equality of the two communities as set out in the relevant resolutions of the UN Security Council: for a state with a single sovereignty, single citizenship and single international personality.

[56]https://en.wikipedia.org/wiki/2018_Cyprus_gas_dispute

ALAS TO THE LOSERS

The arrogant words: "Alas to the losers" of the Gaul leader, Vrennos, to the defeated Romans in 387 BC, are lessons for all losers. The Romans had agreed to pay the Gauls a quantity of gold. When they put the gold on the scale as had been agreed, Vrennos added his sword to the side of his weights so that the Romans had to give more gold. Vrennos replied with the famous dictum, "Vae victims" (Alas to the losers) to the Romans' protest. In other words, those who have had the misfortune of being defeated must suffer the consequences of their mistakes and defeat.

We heard about the same words from the Turkish Prime Minister following their invasion in 1974 when he stated: "The Cyprus problem was solved in 1974".

We live the consequence of our loss when we see the Turkish flag spread in the heart of the Pentadaktylos (mountains), that the repeated prolonged negotiations of more than fifty years have failed to remove.

Some may consider that admitting our loss is a form of defeatism. Of course, we can mimic the ostrich and stick our heads in the occupied soils to not see what is going on around us. We can continue to live in our emotional world as with the "Great Idea" dream. We can live in the hope that the "Blond Race" will come to our aid and believe the prophecies of Turkey's demise.

In the business world, a good manager aims to maximize profit. However, when the company suffers losses, the aim is to minimize the loss.

When I first heard the story of Buridán's donkey, I was impressed. My late Professor John Timmons, at Iowa State University, an authority on international agricultural policy, wanted us to know that in all creation, only man can evaluate his choices and choose the option that will maximize his benefit or minimize his losses.[57] The story is as follows:

Buridán's donkey was equally hungry and thirsty. He was placed midway between a haystack and a bucket of water; he died of hunger and thirst because he couldn't make a rational decision between the hay and the water. He starved to death!

In our current situation, i.e., the status quo, it is always one option: to hang on until the conditions for an acceptable solution change in our favor. Besides, we are well enough as things are.

Cyprus is now a de facto divided state. Turning a blind eye and ignoring the fact that the invasion and continued occupation created a new reality, we live in our illusory world. All indications are that we cannot overturn the conditions imposed on us by the invasion. This was an obligation of the guaranteeing powers of England and Greece to do, but not only did they not do so, but instead cooperated in imposing a new Constitutional regime in Cyprus, in violation of the

---

57 Buridán's ass is an illustration of a paradox in philosophy in the conception of free will. It refers to a hypothetical situation wherein a donkey that is equally hungry and thirsty is placed precisely midway between a stack of hay and a pail of water.

Treaty of Guaranty, which explicitly states:[58]

> *Greece, Turkey, and the United Kingdom taking note of the undertakings of the Republic of Cyprus set out in Article I of the present Treaty, recognize and guarantee the independence, territorial integrity, and security of the Republic of Cyprus, and also the state of affairs established by the Basic Articles of its Constitution. Greece, Turkey, and the United Kingdom likewise undertake to prohibit, so far as concerns them, any activity aimed at promoting, directly or indirectly, either union of Cyprus with any other State or partition of the Island.*

We do not need Constitutionalists to explain what this article of the Guarantee Treaty stipulates. However, as citizens of the Republic of Cyprus, we should demand at least compensation for our damage. Their failure to comply with the Treaty defined the responsibilities they assumed in

Since the paradox assumes the ass will always go to whichever is closer, it dies of both hunger and thirst since it cannot make any rational decision between the hay and water. The paradox is named after the 14th-century French philosopher Jean Buridán, whose philosophy of moral determinism satirizes. Although the illustration is named after Buridán, philosophers had discussed the concept earlier, notably Aristotle who used the example of a man equally hungry and thirsty.

[58]https://www.mfa.gr/images/docs/kypriako/treaty_of_guarantee.pdf

signing this Guarantee.

In the meantime, as the years of the existing situation go on, now for almost fifty years, time cements the territorial and institutional division of the two communities while lengthy negotiations for a solution that *'must be operational and in line with United Nations resolutions' are not reached.* In the meantime, Turkey is increasing its influence in the occupied territories, both militarily, economically, and culturally.

If this stalemate remains, many Greek and Turkish Cypriots believe that whichever "here and now" solution will prevent the risk of partition. But the "any solution" might prevent partition at most only temporarily, but it is too late to prevent it in the long run.

If we put water in our wine for a moment to adopt a moderate stand, setting aside "principles" such as "just solution," "human rights," "majority rule," and accept a retreat, as painful as that may be, and settle for the proposed loose federal arrangement, a serious and thorny issue of security remains. Security is an issue of overriding importance to both communities, and it has proved to be the stumbling block on which all the attempts to find a solution have faltered. A critical provision of the 1960 Treaty of Guarantee is the Guarantors' Powers' right for unilateral intervention to protect the Cyprus Constitutional Order, a provision invoked by Turkey in the 1974 invasion. However, Turkey subsequently violated the provision by then occupying 36%

of the landmass of Cyprus.[59]

In Cyprus, lives were lost, people were uprooted, crimes were committed on both sides, and atrocities were committed whose memories are still with us. A solution – similar to the Zurich agreement, which the two sides accept, but where the attitude of *"I win you lose"* prevails, will collapse with tragic consequences for Cyprus and its people. This can happen at any time by a minor misunderstanding or an incident of violence that escalates to a major confrontation and the collapse of the emerging State.

I am afraid that such happenings are real in the rushing to establish the BBF and should be avoided. The BBF is promoted as a solution for Cyprus's reunification, but it sanctions the existing partition, espousing the Zurich arrangements' rationale. That is racist, divisive, and unworkable, and assuredly expensive. Reunification is certainly the craving of the Cypriots as expressed in the lament of a poem composed by the Turkish Cypriot poet and activist, Nese Yasin, with music arranged by the Greek Cypriot composer, Marios Tokas, where the song's chorus grieves:

"My country has been divided into two; which half should I love?"[60]

---

[59]Turkey occupies the northern one-third of the island, around 36 percent of the territory. The United Nations-controlled Green Line is a buffer zone that separates the two and it takes up about 4 percent. Lastly, two areas—Akrotiri and Dhekelia—remain under British sovereignty for military purposes, collectively forming the Sovereign Base Areas of Akrotiri and Dhekelia (SBA). The SBAs are located on the southern coast of the island and together encompass 254 km2 , or 2.8 percent of the island..

[60] https://www.youtube.com/watch?v=AYO_Xy55Oo4

In the experience we have gone through and the attitudes that we have inherited towards each other and within the prevailing geopolitical conditions of the region in which our country is located, I believe it is impossible to achieve viable reunification at this time. The sense of mutual insecurity, suspicion, and in some circles, deep-rooted intolerance is not a solid basis for peaceful cohabitation and cooperation.

A blatant example of intolerance is the Greek Cypriot community's recent refusal to accept a shelter for orphaned children from war-torn neighboring countries.

Reunification and peaceful cohabitation cannot be achieved by constitutional provisions and regulations mandated by laws from above. As Dale Kanreki says, "anyone whose opinion has changed despite his will, neither his opinion has changed nor his head." For Cyprus's sustainable reunification to be achieved, a cultural awakening is needed that takes us from confrontation and suspicion to cooperation and trust.

We should listen to Apostle Paul's clear message when he wrote in his Letter to the Galatians (3:28), *"There is neither Jew nor Gentile, neither slave nor free, nor is there male and female, for you are all one in Christ Jesus."* In our situation, we should be adding: *"neither Greek Cypriot nor Turkish Cypriot."* It is indeed regrettable that the Church has ignored this spiritual heritage.

We are not ready for peaceful coexistence currently. The reunification needs to be built on a foundation where the two communities accept each other with respect and love, not as an opportunity for exploitation and political gain at the other community's expense.

Our current strategy should focus on an interim transitional solution, which leads to the desired reunification in the long term. Such a transitional solution should embrace the following two pillars:

- Decentralization of Governance, and

- Introduction of provisions of incentives, arrangements, and structures, eliciting, over time, the future unification.

In practice, this means that we must accept some form of administrative autonomy for the "Turkish Republic of Northern Cyprus," with territorial and other elements.

While the two communities will manage their own house as they wish, reunification policies will have to be implemented.

Most Cypriots believe that Greek Cypriots and Turkish Cypriots can work with each other if there are no foreign interventions.

In this arrangement, the two states are members of the European Union, where borders are abolished within the European Acquis provisions. Innovative mechanisms are introduced to foster cooperation and trust between the communities, directing ethnocentrism to constructive pursuits away from suspicion and confrontation. There is such a need for reforms, particularly in education on both sides, to foster the spirit of cooperation, understanding, and tolerance. The European orientation of the whole of Cyprus will, in time, lessen Turkey's control of the North.

Germany is an example of a country that has been reunited after 41 years of dismemberment. Today it is a single and prosperous country.

Of course, one can say that in the case of Germany, there was national homogeneity, which is not the case in Cyprus.

But in Germany, there was ideological heterogeneity, which is worse than racial discrimination.

The years-long isolation of the Turkish Cypriots from the international community has led to their dependence on Turkey, which increased over time. A courageous gesture from the Greek-controlled Republic of Cyprus would be timely and likely to be received with appreciation from the North. One such gesture could be for the Republic of Cyprus to undertake policies targeted to equate the standard of living of both sides [GNP per capita in 2018 in the Turkish North was $14,942, a mere half of the $28,341 of the Greek South]. The casinos' proceeds and the gas fields' exploitation can fund such unification incentives, minimizing their burden on the Cypriot citizens.

An especially important unifying element that has not been utilized: The scientific analysis of the two communities' DNA in Cyprus shows that the genetic code of Greek Cypriots and Turkish Cypriots is the same. In contrast, the Turkish Cypriots' genetic code has nothing to do with that of Turks, whose DNA reflects their Mongolian origins. This scientific truth has unfortunately not, as of now, been embraced as a unifying element.

BUT TO RENOUCE OUR GREEK ANCESTRY?

Many Greek Cypriots will oppose accepting the Turkish compatriots as equal partners with legitimate claims on Cyprus.

The goal of Union with Greece has touched generations of Greek Cypriots, leading to sacrifices and heroic deeds over centuries.

As an extension of the Great Idea, the Union [Ένωσης] was an act of an administrative nature, a geographical integration of us with the national corpus, Greece.

Such a geographical Union is only one and the weakest form of our national rehabilitation, in my estimation. Much stronger is the bond of the spiritual, emotional Union, a Union of which no power can deprive us. The aim should be the Union with the eternal Greek spirit, not with Greece's rotten political establishment. The union of the bonds of the Hellenic soul with Greece, the emotional connection with Greece, the idea as a motherland and the way of life, Greece, the mother of Western Civilization. Union with Greece blends the Orthodox Faith with the Parthenon's shining light, democracy, and freedom, with human rights and culture. Ethos: Greece is for humanity what the heart and mind are for the body. We bond with the Greece of Goethe, Byron, and Eliot.

Such a Union of the Cyprus Hellenes with Mother Greece reaffirms our Greek identity. It obliges us to preserve and resist all kinds of erosion that undercut our millennia's spiritual bond with Hellenism, resisting attempts to falsify history and alter our Greek national identity.

The Greeks' most admirable characteristic, said Churchill, who admired their bravery during the Second World War, is that the whole world fought them over the centuries. They are constantly fighting among themselves. Neither the outsiders nor themselves have been able to eliminate them. Indeed, it is true that despite our infighting, we have survived to this day. Still, the national division brought us great national misfortunes, including the Cyprus tragedy.

We ended up in the predicament that we find ourselves today, having lost our way like the frogs of the myth. They were bouncing happily in the green meadow, happy in bliss and well-being. Suddenly, they fell into a deep well. At first, they were pleased by the refreshing coolness of the water. But when they realized where they had fallen, they asked each other. "And now how are we going to get out of here?"

As I reminded the reader earlier in this writing, the study of history without reflection and, above all, without becoming a beacon of guidance for the future is a dull narrative of events not worth studying.

We Cypriots declare we are Greeks, but how often have we looked at the wisdom of Pythagoras coming to us from the 6th century BC? Even if late, let us listen to Pythagoras and undertake the self-criticism, which was a daily practice for his students.

"When, how, and why did I commit a major offense?"

In other words, we should ask how come we are in such a predicament and who is to be blamed. Admitting our mistakes is painful, but it is a more serious mistake not to acknowledge them.

EPILOGUE

The author's personal views for the causes of the long-lasting Cyprus problem presented in this book can be recapped simply as follows:

- A most important cause of the Cyprus problem's origin and endurance despite the continuous efforts for a solution has been the absence of leaders endowed with insight, vision, and selflessness.

- The choice of armed violence grounded on intolerant ethnocentrism with the Church in the lead was a wrong strategy.

What should be done in the circumstances that we find ourselves, like Odysseus' comrades, who perished because of their own imprudence?

The wise Socrates gives the answer «Καθεύδοντες διατελείτε αν, ει μη τινά άλλον ο Θεός επιπέμψοιε υμίν κηδόμενος υμών».

"We will remain asleep forever unless God has mercy on us and sends us somebody else to take us out from where we threw ourselves."

—Plato, *The Apology of Socrates.*

ABBREVIATIONS

EAC	Electricity Authority of Cyprus
AKEL	People Worker Party
BBF	Bi-zonal Bi-communal Federation
EΔMA	United Democratic Rebuilding Front
EΔON	*United Democratic Youth Organization*
EEC	European Economic Community
EOKA	National Organization of Cypriot Fighters
USA	United States of America
NATO	North Atlantic Treaty Organization
UN	United Nations
ΠEK	Pancyprian Farmers Union
ΠEO	Pancyprian Labor Federation
SEATO	Southeast Asia Treaty Organization
ΣEK	Confederation of Cyprus Workers
CIA	Central Intelligence Agency
TMT	Turkish Resistance Organization (Türk Mukavemet Teşkilatı)

MAP OF CYPRUS

MAP OF CYPRUS

1. Spilia Village, in the Troodos mountain range where Digenis had his headquarters before moving to Limassol.

2. Chloraka. Grivas Digenis arrived secretly on the island and landed on the deserted shore of "Aliki" near Chloraka north of Paphos, the night of 10 November 1954.

3. Avgorou Village. A decisive meeting with a shepherd.

4. Detention Camp Kokinorimethias

5. Detention Camp Pylas

The districts of:

- Nicosia
- Famagusta
- Larnaca
- Kyrenia
- Paphos

▨ The British Bases   ■ United Nations Buffer Zone

ANNEX ONE

Photographs

BROTHERS

PRISONERS 722

DAFNIS SMILING

DAFNIS AND MAROULLA

DAFNIS'S FUNERAL

WITH FELLOW PRISONERS

ANNEX TWO

Dear friends, associates, and fellow freedom fighters of my dear brother and best friend, Dafnis,

Age and Parkinson's have made difficult my presence at this important event, but I am full with you in spirit.

I thank Thales, the very worthy son of Dafnis and of dear Maroulla, as well as their daughters Lydia and Louisa, for the flawless preparation of today's gathering. I also welcome Dora Panagides, who traveled from distant Myanmar (formerly Burma) for this event, whose presence reminds me of how she is like her father in her values and career. I recall that recently from this room, Thales launched his pioneering book "Odyssey to the Heart," where he reveals the way to a happy life with an engaging and creative narrative. You make our whole family proud. Dafnis always said that his wonderful children we owe to their mother Maroulla. Something that, as an objective observer, I totally agree!

Also, a big thank you goes to Leonidas Leonidou for his important contribution in preparing the book's publication. I look forward to his help with the English version to become accessible beyond Cyprus and Greece.

Thales asked me to share some brotherly experiences with Dafnis, which is difficult to do in ten minutes from such rich and multifaceted content.

I begin with Dafnis, the beekeeper, an activity that he mentions in the book when he asks for a bank loan for hives. Every Spring, we started the extermination of the honeybee eating wasps using insecticides such as DDT and Agent Orange. We started from our orchard (today's KEAN) walking all the way to the Sfalansiotisha Monastery to identify and destroy the wasp nests. Even though we wore masks, we could not avoid inhaling some of the poisons the insecticide cloud created by our intervention. That probably maybe the origins of my Parkinson's!?

Dafnis was eight years older than me, and with our father aging and ill, Dafnis was not only a brother but also like a father and a friend.

Our family's participation in the liberation struggle of 1955-59 brought us together even more. For example, when he was sending me on missions such as the taking from our home to Christakis Tryfonides' house, bombs hidden in a vegetable-covered basket, on my way, passing on my bike in front of the police station of St. Nicholas. My arrest would have meant hanging.

On his initiative and thanks to Dafnis' contacts, I left Cyprus in September 1956 with a scholarship to study in America. Later I realized that with this gesture, Dafnis aimed to keep his younger brother alive to continue the Panagides family. It was a wise move as the danger to our family was ever-present as when an auxiliary policeman, during one of our home searches, began to follow the cable to the hideout of the EOKA leader General Grivas Digenis who was hiding in our home. Miraculously he did not reach the end, as the English Commander at the nick of time whistled the end of the operation! Thus, our family was saved from joining the other martyrs on the altar of Cypriot Hellenism.

My pride and appreciation for Dafnis made me believe that he knew everything. So when as a Member of Parliament (MP), he came on an official visit to America, he visited me at Iowa State University in Ames, where I was at the end of my doctoral studies. He tells me, "this is an opportunity to attend a University class now that I am here because when I had to be at a university, I was the guest of Queen Elizabeth at the detention Centre of Kokkinotrimithia."

Fulfilling Dafnis' wish, I arranged for him to attend my class of econometrics! He gave me the impression that he liked this experience. Only after some time did he confess to me, "I understood nothing"! Our dear mother, Maria, known as Konomissa, also came to Ames to visit Dafnis' family and have surgery in 1969. There she left her last breath.

Dafnis' Ames visit marked his family and career. In his 30s, he enrolled at ISU, starting from freshman to Ph.D. He only did not complete the thesis since the invitation to become the General Manager of the Phassouri Plantation with a well-paying job and a house, and returning to his beloved Cyprus, was very attractive. Dafnis and his whole family stayed in Ames for eight years, and where our dear Thales was born. Along with my wife, our dear Joy Caldwell, and her parents, Dr. Marion and Lucille Caldwell helped the family to settle in Ames, which Maroulla remembered as happy and creative years. We also owe Joy the renovation of our house in Kalo Chorio, where Dafnis was born in 1929. It was when cousin Nikos [Papasolomos] ran to give the good news to Solomon Panagides, a teacher at Ag Yiannis, roaring: "Uncle, uncle my aunt gave birth to a fearless lad."

Two incidents of his stay in the United States reveal Dafnis' values.

After my Ph.D. studies, I went to Brazil with the University of California Berkeley program with the Brazilian Institute of Economic and Social Research (IPEA). Dafnis, a student still in Ames, calls me one day and started talking to me about a classmate who needed information and statistics about Brazil. Phone calls then were expensive. I asked, "Dafnis, why so much effort to help this gentleman." Dafnis, after a short pause, replied: "He's English, you know, we must help him." Dafnis Panagides replied, helping an Englishman when we remembered that the English imprisoned him for three years and tortured him. He remained true to the biblical calling *"But I tell you, love your enemies and pray for those who persecute you"* (Matthew 5:44). This demonstration of his deep Christian faith is something that is also shown in the book.

Another incident shows how our dear Dafnis was appreciated by political leaders.

One day when he was with us in Washington in 1974 on his way to Cyprus soon after the Turkish invasion. In downtown Washington, D.C., on K Street, he met the then Governor of the State of Iowa, his friend Governor Harold Hughes. The Governor, in seeing Dafnis, embraced him, and both of them were seen kneeling on the sidewalk with Hughes praying for the good of Cyprus!

This was my dear brother and friend Dafnis Panagides - His memory is eternal. Αιωνία του η μνήμη.

ANNEX THREE

THE DEEP RELATIONSHIP BETWEEN ROY CALVOCORESSI AND
DAFNIS PANAGIDES REVEALED IN DP'S TRIBUTE AT ROY'S FUNERAL
IN LONDON, ENGLAND ON 4TH OCTOBER 2012

[Text in blue enrichments by Roy's wife, Elfrida]

Deep feelings of love, respect, and admiration brought us today under the roof of this holy place to express our gratitude and thank you to Roy for all he has done to bring Peace and give us hope in Cyprus.

Our paths crossed in a miraculous way. But after all, Roy's calling was not from secular institutions; neither was Roy called to peacemaking by the powers and the principalities of this world. Like a new Paul, he was chosen by the Holy Spirit, and he devoted his entire life and material wealth to his calling.

In 1964 I was having afternoon tea in a Nicosia café, pondering Cyprus's future after violence erupted between Greeks and Turks, and the newly established Cyprus Republic appeared to be disintegrating. A slim, soft-spoken Englishman, with a twinkle in his eye and a captivating smile, approached me. He handed me a small piece of paper with a name on it, and he asked me if I knew that person and if I could help him get in touch with him. That name was mine! I did not disclose my identity, but I invited him to come with me to Limassol – my hometown – where I would introduce him to Mr. Dafnis Panagides. We Cypriots are, by nature, suspicious people, more so with the English. On our way to Limassol, Roy impressed me with his deep spiritual commitment and passion for peacemaking and reconciliation. I listened carefully to his vision of making Peace by putting the Prince of Peace at the heart of the peacemaking process and by living and practicing Peace ourselves. In fact, even while he was talking, Roy was convinced he was being kidnapped by this unknown man he had trustingly committed himself to, as Dafnis drove around all the back streets until Roy had completely lost his sense of direction! When they finally stopped outside what proved to be his quarry's house, Dafnis' cover was blown when his young nephews rushed out to greet him, shouting "Uncle Dafnis!"!

My original suspicion that most probably under the face of this innocent-looking Englishman, I was in fact in the hands of an experienced Intelligence Service Agent gradually evaporated, and the American CIA rule that says that the more innocent a guy appears to be, the more suspicious you should become of him, simply did not work. That was the beginning of our long friendship, which brought me here today.

Not long after, the first CHIPS Team was at work in the small village of Kidasi. No-one wants a peacemaker, so the first rule is never to talk to either party about making Peace with the other side. But such was the trust that quickly built between them; Dafnis was the first and, for a long time, the only Cypriot whom Roy entrusted with his emerging ideas about the project. As Roy gradually shared with Dafnis the passages from the Bible which talked about Jesus coming to earth to make peace between God and Man and between communities in conflict, Dafnis was able to explain the deeper meanings of the different Greek words for Peace and bring them to life in his very own context of Cyprus. However, to Roy's great disappointment, as soon as he got permission from the authorities to start restoring the citrus trees in Kidasi - of one community that had been virtually destroyed by the other - Dafnis was forced to take refuge in the USA due to his past involvement with Eoka, and Roy was left to struggle alone. Slow communication between continents at that time, and the erratic nature of their frequency, nevertheless did nothing to weaken the unbreakable bonds of their friendship. **At this solemn moment, I put this soil from Kidasi in Roy's grave to keep him company until we all meet again at Jesus's feet.** *The intense sorrow that Dafnis experienced for the loss of such a friend was such that he could not bear at first to enter the house in the UK, which held such memories of Roy and all that they meant to each other. Whenever Roy returned to Cyprus, he always visited Kidasi village, his home, for 8 years. Kidasi was to Roy the epitome of what practical reconciliation can achieve, through patient, sacrificial presence living in the heart of the tension, quietly rebuilding lives, homes, and livelihoods from the ruins of conflict. Dafnis somehow knew that no other soil could have had such significance for Roy, and therefore for his grieving family.*

The soil is a symbol of reconciliation and hope. Reconciliation comes from orchards of Greeks and Turks that the CHIPS team restored and is blended with sweat, tears, and perhaps drops of blood. Hope because unless the seed is buried in the ground, there can be no harvest. The hope of reconciliation will rise from the grave to prosper and to produce abundant fruits.

From that modest beginning, CHIPS expanded worldwide with several projects and has continued to touch and change the lives of thousands.

In peace, Roy was an original thinker, a biblical scholar, a pioneer in Christian Peacemaking. To talk about Roy's originality cannot be done with justice in a short tribute. However, we can highlight some fundamental principles.

Firstly, it is centered on the Trinity, inspired by the Prince of Peace and sustained by God's sacrificial, unselfish, unconditional love in practice. Secondly, it is grass-roots oriented: living and sharing the simple lifestyles of the belligerent parties and demonstrating peacemaking by example, not big words, through an attitude of humility and grace, not an imposition. Received from his wife Elfrida, my spiritual sister, whom we pray the Lord will strengthen and inspire to continue Roy's outstanding work.

These words spoken by Dafnis may go some way to answering the socalled "mystery" of what changed Dafnis' whole outlook and the course of his life, from the mid-1960s until he died. His real, personal faith in Jesus Christ, whose messenger had met him on that mountainside – an apparent shepherd, reading the Bible (!) – and whose question haunted him throughout his internment by the British, grew almost visibly throughout his life and was sustained by those who shared it. Dafnis' years spent in the care and service of others and of God's creation spoke more eloquently than any words, but in discussions with Roy, and on rare occasions when he did use words to express his faith, they came from his heart of love.

Thirdly, the peacemaking process is nourished by prayer, studying the Bible, and the Eucharistic life of the CHIPS team, enabling the team members to bear both sides' enmity, thereby reducing and even removing it.

Roy and Dafnis also shared a very "wicked" sense of humor! Their deep friendship enabled them to tease each other mercilessly, to play tricks on each other, and to use their considerable powers of language to mislead each other in fun! Unlike his wife, Roy developed an enviable ability, born from experience, never to believe that Dafnis would do what he promised until he saw Dafnis doing it. To read their correspondence is to share a good laugh at times. Still, their sensitivity to each other's condition was very apparent, as in touching letters exchanged over a long period after Maroula died. When Roy was near death, Dafnis came over and spent three days beside his bed, unable to believe his dear friend was going before him.

As we pay tribute to our great friend, a practicing Christian, a loving father, a devoted husband, and a committed peacemaker, we ask Roy now that he has become a son of God not to abandon us in his prayers. We promise his example will stay with us, empowering us to follow the path to peace and reconciliation which he first opened. In this spiritual path, we should acknowledge the significant role and support that Roy.

ANNEX FOUR

RECOLLECTIONS OF DAFNIS PANAGIDES
By Professor Eliseos Paul Taiganides

I opened the book by dafnis panagides ΠΙΚΡΟΔΑΦΝΕΣ around 10 am, and I could not put it down until I finished it hours later. There are a lot of surprises, many names are mentioned, opinions. The book is a wonderful history of the odyssey of Dafnis' life in the liberation of Cyprus from the British occupation and its Union with Mother Greece, the politics and political intrigues that followed.

If you are looking for a book on Cyprus's history, you had better look at the links his brother Stahis provides in this Edition. This is the story of an idealist young man, a patriot, a man of principle and faith, who carried out all the tasks for the struggle, except killing, and even went to prison for it.

The peripatetic life of Dafnis, his sincerity in his commitments, his devotion to the liberation of Cyprus, his sticking to political principles of high standards all are impressive and worth emulating.

I met Dafnis Panagides in the 1960s when he escaped Cyprus's chaotic politics to Ames Iowa, Iowa State University, where his brother Stahis was. Stahis and I did our Ph.D. together. In 1963 I served as best man - koumbaros - at his wedding to Joy Caldwell. I recall that when Dafnis walked into the room and greeted me, I felt his empathy and love. His wife, Maroulla, was just as empathetic as Dafnis. One immediately felt a special warmth.

I was fascinated with his adventures, risk-taking, and systematic approach to serving Cyprus independence with Makarios and Grivas as leading architects. I agree that both of them were heroes of the Independence war, but also the ones and mainly responsible for the failures that ensued after 1960 and the Island's present predicament. Both of them were arrogant and authoritarian.

In 2017, at Dafnis' recommendation, I went to Cyprus to advise the Government on how to manage hotel waste. When the following dinner one night, we attended a theatrical presentation of the Crucifixion of Christ by the Metropolitan Opera at a local theater. It was Holy Thursday. At the end of that realistic performance of the Crucifixion drama, it seemed that almost everyone in the theater came to say hello to Dafnis.

Among his many contributions is the founding of "The Cyprus Sustainable Tourism Initiative", to develop a sustainable tourism approach for an island that received 3.98 million tourists in 2019.

In recognition of his contributions to the environment and the country, Limassol's Municipal Council in 2019 named one of the city's Parks "Dafnis Panagides."

*https://www.facebook.com/neapolislemesos/
posts/20902293 77942363/f*

These are memories of my brotherly friend, Dafnis Panagides, and some of the reasons that this book is a must-read, not only for learning about the recent history of Cyprus, an island in the unsettled Eastern Mediterranean, an unsinkable aircraft carrier, but most importantly to see how an individual can be an agent for good.

I understand a film based on Dafnis' incredible life under the direction of renowned Greek cinematographer Costas Ferris, is in preparation with this book's title, "CYPRUS: ISLAND IN THE STORM: An individ ual encircled by violence becomes a voice for reconciliation and peace." I look forward to its international release expected in 2022.

I am grateful to my Koumbaros, Stahis Panagides, Dafnis' brother, and the Dorrance Publishing Company for making "Bitter Leaves of Laurel" available in this excellent English Edition.

Eliséos Paul Taiganides
Ελισσαίος Paul Ταϊγανίδης
Author: "ΗΔίκητουΣωκράτη'"" TheTrial of Socrates
Professor of Environmental Engineering [retired],

ANNEX FIVE

LETTERS BETWEEN ACHESON AND GREEK PRIME MINISTER, PAPANDREOU, SUMMER 1964

ACHESON PLAN 2

The Greek government declined the first Acheson Plan, and so a second version was submitted.

The Turkish base area simply be leased to Turkey for an agreed period of years - 50 was suggested as reasonable - instead of being ceded as sovereign Turkish territory.

The boundary of the base area on the Karpas Peninsula would be a line drawn north and south just west of the village of Komi Kebir (thus reducing the area considerably). Alternatively, Mr. Acheson suggested that the line could be drawn based on military considerations after study by the Supreme Allied Commander for Europe.

The special provisions and guarantees for the Turkish-Cypriots would be modified from those proposed in Acheson Plan me to eliminate the special areas containing a Turkish-Cypriot majority which would have been treated under the first plan as moderate administrative units. Instead, it was suggested that at least two of the eparchies into which Cyprus might be divided under Greek rule would always be headed by Turkish-Cypriot eparchs. These eparchies would always be those containing a substantial Turkish-Cypriot population. In the eparchies containing such a substantial Turkish-Cypriot population, the administrative staff, police, etc. would always contain a substantial proportion of Turkish-Cypriot officials and employees.

Instead of the central Turkish-Cypriot administration in Nicosia which was proposed in Acheson Plan I, there would be a high official in the central Government of Cyprus, under the chief Greek administrator, who would be provided with a staff and would be charged with looking after the rights and welfare of all Turkish-Cypriots. This official would advise and assist Turkish Cypriots, receive, and investigate complaints about discriminatory treatment or failure to give guaranteed rights, and could appeal to the courts or central government of Greece in case of need.

The special guarantees or minority rights envisaged in the first plan, such as those provided by the Treaty of Lausanne and the European Convention on Human Rights, would be retained.

Similarly, the proposed International Commissioner appointed by the U.N. would be part of the second plan as of the first.

Letter from Dean Acheson to Greek Prime Minister George Papandreou, July 26, 1964

"In the previous talks I recommended to the Greek Government that, within the framework of a solution which it might be possible to find regarding the Cyprus problem, either for an independent Cyprus or of a Cyprus directly connected with Greece, certain rights of self-administration must be secured for the Turkish minority.

The minority must also have full legal safeguards of acknowledged human and minority rights, of the type that are defined in the Lausanne Treaty. To give to Turkey and to the Turkish Cypriots the assurance that these arrangements will be applied and will be absolutely respected, I had proposed that this would be done by an international supervisory representative or group. You were kind enough to inform me that the Prime Minister had agreed, in principle, to these proposals, and I consider this as an important step forward to the direction of the peace objective, which we are trying to reach.

I do not think it is necessary or desirable to try to define now the details of the provisions of the minority rights, which must be included in the final solution.

These can be derived from the Lausanne Treaty, the Declaration of Human Rights of the United Nations, and other known texts. Without doubt there must be amendments to correspond to the circumstances which prevail in Cyprus. In any case the task of drafting such provisions will take a long time and needs more staff than what you and we have at our disposal. The agreement for the exact provisions which must be included must, by necessity, be agreed between Greece and Turkey. It would, however, be useful for you and the Prime Minister, if I try to give you some more concrete ideas regarding the administrative arrangements which I have in mind, and the aspects of the plan of supervision.

As I foresee it is likely that there will be one or two, perhaps three areas in the island in which the Turks will have the majority or almost the majority.

For the time being, the Turkish sectors of Nicosia and the area which extends to the north, towards the Kyrenia range is one example of such an area. These areas would be treated as separate geographical units for administrative purposes, in the framework of the general Government organization of the administration of the island. They could have their own special local administrations which would be directed and applied by Turkish Cypriots.

If the island is annexed to Greece, these units could be called districts on condition that the District Commissioner and the largest part of his staff would always be Turkish Cypriots and would have a considerable degree of local autonomy.

Their functions would include the collection of taxes, either for local or national purposes, the cost of the local expenditure for schools, local systems 'of supplying water for domestic purposes, roads, drainage systems and other public works. They could also include the administration of the local police forces and the general administration of justice. They must have all the jurisdiction of municipal and district governments in every respect and substantial freedom should be given in the administration of their affairs with the minimum possible interference of the Central Government.

As I understand it, the organization of the Greek administration must be such that would permit considerable flexibility in this sector. The Dodecanese, for instance, are administered in a somewhat different manner than the mainland of Greece. These local governments would not constitute a state within a state. In the last analysis they would be responsible to a superior authority, which may be the central government of an independent Cyprus, the supreme representative of the Greek state in Cyprus, or the Government of Greece in Athens. The district commissioner would be appointed in the usual manner by the central authority on condition that he must be a Turkish Cypriot. If the district should have a substantial number of Greek Cypriots it would be logical for the police and certain other administrative organs to include Greek Cypriot employees in the Turkish majority.

A system of mixed police patrols could be used, for instance, in certain areas (this would also be useful in areas outside the Turkish Districts).

In the rest of the island, where the Turkish Cypriots would continue to be a small minority, a different arrangement would be necessary. I suggest that there could be a central Turkish Cypriot administration in Nicosia, which would exercise control on the Turkish Cypriots only, in most of the same activities which the local authorities would have in the Turkish districts already referred to above.

One way in which this could be done would be to agree on the boundaries of the Turkish sectors of the largest towns and to define the villages which are Turkish as well as where the Turks are in the majority. These would be under the jurisdiction of the Turkish administration in Nicosia, which will have at its head a district Commissioner, who would supervise the election or appointment of the local authorities, the administration of the police and other public functions, and of the lower courts for the hearing of cases of personal status, civil cases between Turks, criminal prosecutions against Turks and similar cases of purely Turkish interest. Similarly, the corresponding authorities in the separate geographical districts, the organization would be answerable to the central authority of the island, whichever it might be, but it would have a substantive degree of administrative freedom. It is obvious that many aspects of this plan should be developed and be agreed by negotiations between the interested parties. My suggestions are not intended to be in any way definitive or exclusive.

The application of the safeguards of human rights, the right to use Turkish special courts in certain kinds of cases and other similar privileges would be extended to all Turkish Cypriots, despite the fact, that for any reason, some may not come under the direct jurisdiction of either of the of two Government units which I have recommended. I presume that by agreement, the legislation of the central authority of the state, there will be a special section of the legislation which would be applicable equally for all the Turkish Cypriots citizens on subjects which require special legal treatments for national, religious and customary reasons. All Turks will, of course, be citizens of the state and will have the same rights and privileges with all other inhabitants.

Despite the fact that the Greek record in the area of minorities is good, the history of the Cyprus problem and the feelings which have been created as a result of the disturbances of the last 7 months in Cyprus, have convinced me that it will be necessary in the arrangements to have special machinery to safeguard the application of such rights as would exist and the self-Government of the minority. The logical manner to achieve this, in my opinion, would be the United Nations or the International Court to appoint an international Commissioner or a commission The Commissioner or commission would be in the island and would have jurisdiction and the responsibility of the supervision of compliance with the special status and of the rights of the Turkish Cypriots. There are precedents for this in the case of Danzig and the Soar, in the interval between the first and second world war".

ON 20TH OF AUGUST 1964, DEAN ACHESON SENT THE FOLLOWING LETTER TO PRIME MINISTER PAPANDREOU:

Dear Mr. Prime Minister:

May I begin this letter by expressing deepest appreciation of the help you have given to our work here in Geneva by your own constant attention and thought and by permitting Mr. Rossides to join in our efforts. Today the President has informed me of the urgency which he believes imminent Soviet involvement in the Cyprus problem has imparted to our work, and because of it has asked me to let you know our joint view that only a little while is left in which a settlement can be made and to give you my own views, which he has endorsed, of the general nature of the settlement which seems to me possible and fair. I know from our conversations with Mr. Rossides that you are impressed as we are here of the danger, which the Russian moves have intensified, that Cyprus will fall under Communist influence and of the farreaching efforts which this will have upon the political and power situation in the Eastern Mediterranean. I am sure we agree that the danger gives Turkey and Greece a common interest far transcending the exact lines on a map to be drawn in reaching an agreement. The problems presented by both sides in reaching a settlement are political and it is from that point of view that I approach them.

I am prepared to apply the utmost pressure and persuasion to get that Turks to give up any claim for sovereign territory on Cyprus, to reduce the dimensions of their requirements for a military base on the Karpas Peninsula and to settle the rights of minorities along the lines which I have discussed with Mr. Rossides and which I can translate into a draft to be available tomorrow. Specifically, I would urge the Turks to limit their plan to a lease for 50 years for that part of the Karpas Peninsula running from its north-easterly end to a line drawn north and south just west of Komi Kebir. I am persuaded from the study which I have made of the situation with the aid of military advisers that there is a sound military justification for such a base in the defense of the approaches to the Turkish mainland and in the defense of the base itself from surprise attack. It is quite possible that to draw the Western line of this area as have suggested would present a political problem to you at this time This problem could be avoided by leaving the line undrawn, to be supplied after military study by the Supreme Allied Commander for Europe, with the assurance by the Government of Greece that if the line should be drawn as indicated, it would be accepted. Indeed, the willingness of the Government of Greece to enter such a settlement might be indicated to me without entering any present direct commitment to the Government of Turkey. With this assurance I would do my best and believe I could succeed, in obtaining the agreement of the Government of Turkey not to intervene to prevent or to demand prior intergovernmental agreement before the achievement of enosis between Greece and Cyprus. Without something of this sort, the Turks would surely believe themselves to be faced with having their treaty rights almost contemptuously destroyed and themselves faced with the alternatives of unconditional enosis or unconditional independence for a Cyprus under communist domination. What I have suggested will present the gravest difficulties for the leaders of both Greece and Turkey and for the peoples they lead. But I am confident that, in the face of imminent common peril, each nation can find unity at home in support of solutions which look beyond momentary controversy, to the fundamental security and welfare of great Hellenic and Turkish states and support abroad by the grand alliance of free states against interference with their execution. May I request, my dear Prime Minister, the early return to Geneva of Mr. Rossides to help us to this solution.

Sincerely yours,

Dean Acheson

LETTER FROM PRIME MINISTER PAPANDREOU TO DEAN ACHESON, AUGUST 22, 1964

Dear Mr. Acheson:

Ambassador Labouisse had the kindness to hand me yesterday your letter of August 20th and to inform me that your proposals have been approved by the Government of the United States.

I wish to express my warmest thanks for the admirable efforts you are making to find a solution to the Cyprus problem: a solution which will avert war and will restore relations between allies, members. And we sincerely desire to assist your efforts in interest of Greece, of free world and peace. I fully share your view that "the danger gives Turkey and Greece a common interest for transcending exact lines on a map to be drawn..."

Therefore, yesterday I assured Ambassador Labouisse that we accepted "in principle" your proposals.

However, I deem it necessary to draw your attention upon a fundamental fact. I have the impression that the Government of the United States may believe that if Greece accepted a plan for a solution to the Cyprus question, the problem could be solved. This is not correct. Certainly, our decision is of vital importance. But. Finally, the decisive word belongs to the leadership and people of Cyprus which is now an independent state.

The Turkish Government does not face such a problem as regards Turkish Cypriots who are subservient to Ankara. The problem exists only for us. If we accepted a solution which Cyprus would reject as unjust, the situation would deteriorate. In such an event we may be certain that Cypriots will continue their struggle and seek aid from wherever it will be possible to obtain it: we already know from where they will ask and obtain it. For this important reason, the conditions of an agreement should not be excessive so that they may be acceptable to Cyprus and thus lead us on a peaceful and definite settlement instead of coming to an insuperable deadlock.

As I informed Ambassador Labouisse yesterday, our Minister of National Defense, Mr. Garoufalias, went to Cyprus with the dual purpose of postponing conclusion of an agreement with Moscow and sounding out the policies of Archbishop Makarios. Mr. Garoufalias returned today from his mission, he succeeded in preventing, for time being, Mr. Kyprianou, the Foreign Minister of Cyprus, from leaving for Moscow tomorrow, as originally planned. He also succeeded in postponing the visit of the Archbishop to Cairo to meet President Nasser. The postponement of both trips is temporary depending on the development of the situation. Mr. Garoufalias also ascertained views of President Makarios. The Archbishop rejects absolute granting of any base either to NATO or Turkey. He also envisages the abolition of British bases.

We would of course prefer obtaining Enosis without giving anything in exchange. This would have been fair since Turkish minority will acquire full protection under Greek administration as Moslem minority enjoys in Thrace for many years. Moreover, security of Turkey would be completely safeguarded as Cyprus becoming part of Greece would belong to NATO. Besides, since Cyprus was sold by Turkey to Great Britain the former never had any base in the island for security of Turkish state. Neither did agreements of Zurich grant Turkey such a right. We recognize, however, that under present conditions, for psychological reasons as well as for reasons of prestige, it will be difficult for Turkey to consent to union of Cyprus with Greece without obtaining something in exchange. Therefore, we are ready to offer special guarantees for Turkish Cypriots without impairing Greek sovereignty and unity of the state. We would also accept to grant lease of an area for a logical period for the installation of a Turkish base.

Greece could support the idea of Turkish base, even if the Archbishop did not agree, and could perhaps convince the great majority of Cyprus people to accept it, provided the dimensions of the base were limited. For instance if they correspond to the extent of British bases in Cyprus. Your proposal, which I understand is the result of strenuous negotiations, exceeds by far the space necessary for establishment of a military base and has a character of limited partition. Unfortunately, we cannot support such a proposal. The difficulty has become greater owing to psychological conditions prevailing in Cyprus following the recent Turkish bombing of civilian population. The climate on the island at this moment is most unfavorable to Turkey and NATO. It is also unfavorable to Greece due to her absence during Turkish aggression.

We understand that you have exhausted all means of persuasion with Turks so that they may reduce their claims. Therefore, I am not addressing to you an appeal to that effect. I confess my distress and disappointment that agreement cannot be reached. It remains now for us to do all we can for maintenance of peace on the island until the next session of the General Assembly of the United Nations to which we commit all our hopes for acceptance of the principle of unrestricted independence including the right to self-determination."

LETTER FROM DEAN ACHESON TO PRIME MINISTER PAPANDREUOU, AUGUST 22, 1964:

My Dear Prime Minister:

Thank you for your letter of August 22nd, replying to mine of August 20th

I deeply regret that you have thought it not politically feasible for the Government of Greece in the present circumstances to accept the proposals which I put to you and to the Government of Turkey.

These proposals seemed to me to embody equitable, realistic, and reasonable arrangements that could form the basis of an agreed solution. I was encouraged to find that my Government in Washington took the same view. However, as you know, the Government of Turkey is finding as much diffi culty in accepting these proposals as you are, although it has not, as I understand it, finally rejected them. It seems clear from the attitude of the Government of Turkey that any other proposals closer to your position would, a fortiori, be unacceptable.

In view of the response to my proposals, there appears to be an impasse at least for the present. I have no further suggestions as to a solution.

I would hope, however, that you and your Government would consider very solemnly the dangerous alternatives to a peaceful settlement.

In the final paragraph of your letter, you say it remains now to work for the maintenance of peace in Cyprus. This surely should be the goal of the Government of Greece and all other Governments concerned. The establishment and maintenance of security on the island and the restoration of normal life for all its inhabitants is the essential prerequisite for avoiding the catastrophe of a military clash between Greece and Turkey. If peaceful conditions prevail, emotional pressures will be greatly reduced. Elemental protection of life and livelihood in Cyprus might produce a new atmosphere in both Greece and Turkey and permit resumption of efforts to reach a wider solution.

During our latest conversations here with Ambassador Nicolaides and Mr. Rossides, I put forward some personal ideas as to what your Government might do to stabilize and normalize the situation on the island. Mr. Rossides has undoubtedly reported these to you, and I hope you will give them consideration. Any harassment of Turkish-Cypriots will end whatever hope remains of a peaceful solution of Cyprus, problems. I shall not say more, but ask you to believe that these words, in a literal sense, represent my most solemn prognosis.

ANNEX SIX

READER REACTIONS TO
CYPRUS: ISLAND IN THE STORM

The thoroughness of Panagides' description of events in Cyprus paints a clear picture of history. His insightful narrative also unmistakably shows us what might have been. Whither Cyprus today? Panagides points us in that direction, too, making this book a must-read!.

—Ambassador Marianne M. Myles

A love story

When we met Dafnis several years ago, he was in the middle of writing this book; he told us how it had become an intense and painful process to re-live the experiences that had occupied such an important part of his life. At this time, he was struggling with broadening his own old positions, becoming more open to seeing Cyprus as one people buffeted by forces beyond its shores. To that end, he arranged for us to meet with people from both sides of the divide and encourage them to continue what he considered an indispensable dialogue.

Dafnis remains unforgettable; his wisdom, his passionate love for all of his country changed us too. We will forever be in his debt and will always remain in love with Cyprus.

—Marta L. Rovira Ph.D. Social Psychology
School Psychologist Fairfax County VA
Public Schools (ret)

and

—Ramón E. Daubon PhD
VP Inter American Foundation (ret)
International Institute for Sustained
Dialogue, Board Member

Many thanks to Stahis Panagides for allowing me to read an early draft of this book in which his brother Dafnis gives us a deeply personal insight into the struggle for freedom in Cyprus, a struggle that required sacrifice, imprisonment, and many acts of violence. In his journey for the freedom of Cyprus encircled by violence and communal conflict between the Greek and Turkish Cypriots, he evolves into an advocate of reconciliation and peace. It's a story that can be told only by someone who lived through it. Panagides' experiences and lessons embraced in the Christian Hellenic values that he shares with modesty and transparency are valuable lessons not only for Cyprus but relevant for the many challenges facing today's world. It is a most valuable read for policymakers and citizens worldwide.

—Richard White,
Former Associate Vice Chancellor for
Communications and Public Affairs
The University of North Carolina at
Chapel Hill

This is a book that every concerned citizen should read, especially in Brazil, to learn from the authors' example how political leaders can serve the public good with patriotism, transparency, and honesty. The reader will learn about the turbulent recent history of this beautiful Island and how its location in the strategic Easter Mediterranean is both a blessing and a curse, making it the target of outsiders, especially these days Turkey, complicating its political life. Dafnis explains how the independence granted in 1960 establishing the Republic of Cyprus with an unworkable constitution broke down with the violent conflict between the Greek and Turkish communities, offering valuable recommendations for achieving reconciliation and peace. It was my privilege to have Dafnis as one of my friends.

—Cesar Augusto De Aguiar, DVM, MSc, MBA
Honorary Consul of the Republic of Cyprus
in São Paulo-Brazil

www.ingramcontent.com/pod-product-compliance
Lightning Source LLC
Chambersburg PA
CBHW040844120626
46547CB00001B/11